Praise for *Improve Your Wri*

When people find out I have written over 30 ~~...~~ ~~...~~ confess to me that they have always wanted to write a book. But wanting to write a book is common – writing a book, less so. Judith Pearson's *Improve Your Writing with NLP* will improve the odds of getting that book within you written. It has strategies that I wish I had known when I was starting out – it would have made writing a book much easier and quicker. If you long to write a book, reading *Improve Your Writing with NLP* can put you one giant step closer.

Bill O'Hanlon, author of *Write is a Verb* and
Becoming a Published Therapist

To be able to write is to have a different kind of voice – one that can share a vision with the world. Judith Pearson offers a means whereby pretty much anyone can find their voice. It is a tribute to what she has done that the question now is not so much, "how do you write?" but, "what do you really want to say?"

Ian McDermott, Founder of International Teaching Seminars and
author of numerous bestsellers including
Principles of NLP, The NLP Coach* and *The Coaching Bible

As the former publisher of *Anchor Point* journal and co-author of several books, I know how daunting it can seem to get your ideas out in a book or article. Judith's book, *Improve Your Writing with NLP*, offers practical and easy-to-follow instructions to help you write imaginatively and effectively, and to stay motivated through a writing project. The book is packed with tips and suggestions that you may not have considered in planning and writing. She also shows how you can use the Dreamer – Realist – Critic strategy as a creative approach to reach your audience. The worksheets included at the end of the book provide a clear guide for thinking through a writing project. In fact, they alone are worth the price of the book.

Tim Hallbom, NLP Author, Developer and Trainer,
NLP and Coaching Institute

The difference between people who succeed at an endeavor and those who do not, is about whether (or not) they implement their great ideas. Judith Pearson's book shows you exactly what you need to do to succeed at writing and enjoy the process. I suggest you read this book, and then close it often in order to do the exercises that will allow you to implement her great strategies. This will guarantee your success! I highly recommend Judith's book.

Shelle Rose Charvet, author of
Wishing, Wanting and Achieving

If you are interested in writing and you want to tap into the genius of the NLP Communication Model, Judith Pearson's new book is just the book for you! Why do I say that? Because here is a solid, NLP-based book that uses and applies many of the very best patterns to bring out your own very best as a writer.

In this book you will find a lot of practical suggestions on how to think about writing, how to organize yourself as you write, how to get yourself into the best mental and emotional states to write, and how to use the three dimensions of the Disney Creative Strategy so that your writing is creative, realistic, and refined.

How do you get in rapport with your readers? Judith shows you how! Using perceptual positions, getting engagement, answering the "what's in it for me?" question. And what if you are not a writer and don't plan to be a writer? Judith quotes me as saying that one of the reasons I write is to learn. In fact, I write to learn and, by writing, I incorporate my learning in my own words. Writing helps me learn. And it can help you learn as well. Bottom line: Go buy this book!

L. Michael Hall, Ph.D., Co-Developer of
Neuro-Semantics and Meta-Coaching,
author of over 45 books in the field of NLP

In *Improve Your Writing with NLP*, Judith Pearson, Ph.D. offers a well-rounded perspective on how to tap the power of NLP to improve your writing skills. She also helps to access the wellspring of creativity and ideas that might be locked up in the far corners of your mind and otherwise be inaccessible to you. In that regard, this book is also about how to improve your thinking with NLP. What's more, this is a hands-on guide, with keen insights, probing questions, and ready-to-use worksheets to propel you along.

Jeff Davidson, "The Work-Life Balance Expert®" and
author of *Breathing Space, Simpler Living*,
and *The 60 Second Innovator*

Engaging! I genuinely enjoyed reading *Improve Your Writing with NLP*. It is an excellent role model for the very thing the book is about ... NLP and Writing! As an editor of a journal, this book is a fantastic reference and I will be adding it to our "must read" list. I would recommend this book to anyone who wants to express their ideas well through writing whilst maintaining a passion for their subject.

Joe Cheal, NLP Master Trainer, author and editor of
Acuity: The ANLP Journal

Judith provides a worthy and valuable guide to a subject which may be challenging to many people, including myself! She shines a light on many of the dark areas experienced when writing, and offers superb and practical advice to overcome these particular challenges. Judith has a gentle and clear way of communicating with us through her book and her NLP applications serve as a practical guide to NLP as well as to writing. Thank you, Judith, for providing such an insightful and useful how-to guide for using NLP to improve my writing.

Karen Moxom, Managing Director,
The Association for NLP – The Association for NLP Professionals

IMPROVE YOUR WRITING WITH NLP

Judith E. Pearson, Ph.D.

Crown House Publishing Limited
www.crownhouse.co.uk
www.crownhousepublishing.com

First published by

Crown House Publishing Ltd
Crown Buildings, Bancyfelin, Carmarthen, Wales, SA33 5ND, UK
www.crownhouse.co.uk

and

Crown House Publishing Company LLC
6 Trowbridge Drive, Suite 5, Bethel, CT 06801-2858, USA
www.crownhousepublishing.com

First printed 2013

British Library Cataloguing-in-Publication Data
A catalogue entry for this book is available from the British Library.

ISBN
ISBN: 978-184590861-4 (print)
ISBN: 978-184590874-4 (mobi)
ISBN: 978-184590875-1 (epub)

LCCN: 2012952426

Printed and bound in the UK by
Gomer Press, Llandysul, Ceredigion

This book is dedicated to John—my sweetheart, husband, soul mate, and closest friend.

Also by Judith E. Pearson, Ph.D.

The Weight, Hypnotherapy and You Weight Reduction Program: An NLP and Hypnotherapy Practitioner's Manual

Why Do I Keep Doing This?!!
End Bad Habits, Negativity, and Stress with Self-hypnosis and NLP

Acknowledgments

Many authors have lamented that the book they produce is never as good as the one they originally envisioned. I always feel that way about my books. Nevertheless, acknowledgments are due to those stalwarts who gave maximum effort and skill to help make this book resemble the one I had in mind.

David Bowman and the staff at Crown House Publishing did more than shepherd this book to publication. They demonstrated patience when unexpected events in my life delayed completion of the manuscript and revisions. They answered my questions and advised me. Mark Tracten, the Crown House U.S. representative, gave helpful recommendations about chapter titles as the draft neared completion.

Although I've never met Richard Bolstad, I've admired him through his books and articles for many years. An article he wrote in *Anchor Point* in 2003 grabbed me. The ideas stayed with me. That single article inspired me to write this book. I thought it only fitting that Richard should write the foreword. I feel honored and grateful that he said yes.

I also thank Dixie Elise Hickman and Sid Jacobson for developing the POWER Process and for publishing *The POWER Process: an NLP Approach to Writing* in 1997. This book revealed to me, for the first time, how a little knowledge of NLP makes writing easier. Sid and Dixie were both generous and gracious in allowing me to include the POWER Process in this book. Mine is one of many lives their work has influenced in a positive way.

I've mentioned many NLP authors throughout the text who have continually taught, inspired, and informed me through their words and accomplishments. Some I've had the good fortune to meet in person; others through phone conversations or via email correspondence. Their insights and knowledge have graced the pages of this book. I acknowledge these authors for their example and the many ways in which they have given of their time, energies, and talents to make the world a better, happier place. I especially thank those who gave me permission to cite their books and articles, quote them, and write about their work.

I thank my husband, John, an author himself, for his continuing support and morale-boosting throughout the project of writing this book. John helped edit these pages and gave suggestions about content. He routinely took over household chores to give me time to write. Sometimes he gave me the quiet, uninterrupted concentration time and space every author needs. He is a generous, decent, caring sweetheart of a guy. I cherish our marriage and a friendship that began over 30 years ago.

Last, I thank you, the reader, for picking up this book and deciding it might be useful to your writing endeavors. You are the person I had in mind as I wrote and revised each sentence.

Author's Note

Wherever I have mentioned experiences or conversations with clients in this book, I have changed the names and consequential details to protect their privacy. Some cases are represented as composites rather than the experience of any one individual.

Foreword

Research shows that many people don't fully read the foreword of a book, so the fact that you are reading this may already be an indication of your interest in the way books are written. Well, I have good news for you. Whether you are an experienced writer who wants to improve the effectiveness and publication rate of your work, or you are someone who is embarking on their first ever writing project, you are in for a treat! This book connected with me in three major ways.

Firstly, I have published a dozen books and hundreds of articles in ten different languages, so writing is one of my passions, and I'm very interested in how to do it well. Secondly, even when I'm not writing, I am a Certified Trainer of NLP (Neuro-Linguistic Programming) which is the methodology that guides much of this book, and I want to learn as much as I can about this amazing field. Thirdly, this is an inspiring book, a book which made me want to begin writing all over again, and so reading it was like a second honeymoon with my writing career.

Now I'm going to tell you in a little more detail about these three connections. Let's start with the last one, because it's the most important to me. Judith Pearson obviously loves writing. Of all the people whose reviews of my books I've read, she's the one person who I know for sure read my book before reviewing it. And her passion for writing is contagious. You will understand that, if you've read one of her other books, and you'll feel it as you read this. Try to resist the temptation to read this whole book in a day (which I did, the first time) or, if you can't, be curious about what it is that makes this "how-to" book so exciting to read. You can learn not only from what Judith tells you about writing, but also from studying and "modeling" *how* she wrote this example.

Judith says, "The most successful writers strive to enrich the lives of others and better the world around them. Successful writers derive pleasure when they inform, entertain, inspire, persuade, and move people to action. They believe in the value of what they produce and consider writing as a means to answer a calling." This book is an invitation to join a great writer in her calling. It reminds me of those times when I wake up in the morning and realize, with gratitude to life, that I am going to be able to write today. This book is a place to soak up that attitude. Finally, with Judith, you will say "Ahh! So *that's* how it feels to be a writer!"

Secondly, Judith knows all the details about what it really takes to make writing a practical reality, and she knows how to explain that to you. Rather than just being a person with a manuscript waiting at the back of your mind, you'll learn how to get published results. Whatever the subject, the format and the context of the writing you decide to do, this book explains how to do it. As a writer, I really checked that this book shows you how to deal with every imaginable challenge, external and internal, that you might face.

There are details about making sure your computer is up to the challenge, finding and expanding on creative ideas for writing, writing a thorough plan of your work in linear sequence and in mindmap format, doing thorough research on your topic, getting yourself to actually put words down on paper, understanding and selling your ideas to your audience, presenting a coherent thesis, and writing with both precision and playful ambiguity as required.

Judith can tell you these things with specific concrete examples from her own life ... right down to showing you the actual cover letter that finally got her a job as a Program Manager/Writer after 70 failed attempts. And then she has concrete, step-by-step exercises that install these skills in your brain and body. Nothing of her success is hidden. If you've got a question about writing, the answer is here somewhere.

The third connection I have with this work is my familiarity with NLP. Most of the creativity and self-management skills that Judith teaches in this book come from that field. Her coverage of these is as exquisite as her coverage of the other writing skills. So much so, that this is also one of the best introductions to NLP I have seen. That makes this book literally two books for the price of one. The book covers the NLP field from its most basic presuppositions, which she shows are also the basic presuppositions of successful writers, to the most advanced processes for changing your state of mind and freeing you up to do what you want to do. This book will not just make you a better writer, it will help you to become a better human being.

There is an image that seems at home with tragic writers such as Fyodor Dostoyevsky and Thomas Hardy, of the writer as a tortured soul who draws on her or his own suffering to write a cry of anguish. *Improve Your Writing with NLP* will show you, instead, how to write words that sing with your joy; how to make your writing projects the perfume of a personal life and a career that is also blossoming.

Judith takes you in depth through the creativity strategy which NLP trainer Robert Dilts modeled from Walt Disney, and the POWER Process for writing, developed by NLP experts Dixie Elise Hickman and Sid Jacobson. She also shares insights from prolific writers in the NLP field, such as L. Michael Hall, about how to keep creativity flowing. NLP practitioners and trainers will also learn from the elegant way that Judith presents NLP, and from the breadth of her knowledge of the field. There is so much here, that we can all expect to learn new NLP skills and new applications of the NLP model. Imagine how much more you could achieve in your career if you added the skill of writing inspirational and persuasive texts. I recommend this book to every NLP trainer and practitioner.

This book, then, is a book for anyone who wants to write, and anyone who wants a better life and would welcome writing as a celebration of that life. It is a book for those who want to learn NLP for the first time and for those who want to fill out their understanding of it and communicate that understanding to others. And above all, it is an opportunity to experience great writing as you learn about it. Enjoy!

Dr Richard Bolstad
NLP Trainer and Author of *Transforming Communication*
Auckland, New Zealand
October 12, 2012

Contents

INTRODUCTION

What Does NLP have to do with Writing?

Have you ever read a book or an article and thought to yourself, "I could have … written that"?

Do you secretly agree when someone tells you that you ought to write a book or article on a topic you know well?

Do you long to see your byline at the top of a magazine page, a screenplay, or on the cover of a book?

Do you have all kinds of topics you'd like to write about buzzing around in your brain, yet you don't know where to begin?

If you answered "yes" to any of these questions, this book will show you how Neuro-Linguistic Programming (NLP) will improve your ability to transport ideas from your head onto the printed page.

Or perhaps your situation is that every time you begin to write, you feel intimidated by that blank page staring back at you. It seems to say, "What's wrong with you? Don't you know how to write?" Then, does your mind fill with so many fears and precautions that you feel as though a dragon is breathing down your neck? If you suffer from writer's block, it's because you start with the wrong mindset. NLP will help you to start writing and keep on writing with the right mindset.

Or maybe you've already tested the waters of writing with reviews, articles, or a blog, and you simply want to learn more about how to smooth out the process and get past the glitches. NLP will help there too.

With a little knowledge of NLP, you can write more creatively, efficiently, and prolifically. With NLP, you can sharpen your edge. In the pages that follow, I promise to teach you how.

One Writer's Path: My Story

If you said "That's me," to any of the above paragraphs, then you are the reader I envisioned for this book. We have something in common. I've known each phase of authorship, from wannabe to actually getting published.

As a teenager, I wrote for the high school newspaper. I scrawled half-finished novels and trite short stories into spiral notebooks. I compulsively kept journals. Then I went to college and got interested in social work, psychology, and counseling.

Years later, while getting my doctorate in counseling, I submitted a term paper on nutrition and mental health. My instructor liked it. As I was finishing up an exam, he called me over to his desk. He held my term paper in his hand. "You ought to publish this," he said. "Let me co-author with you to show you how." The very word, "publish" seemed to lift me three feet off the ground! My teenage dreams of being an author were revived in an instant!

Professor Thomas J. Long and I published "Counselors, Nutrition, and Mental Health" in the *Personnel and Guidance Journal* in 1982. From the moment I saw my byline, I was hooked. I couldn't stop thinking of all the things I wanted to say on a printed page. I knew I had to keep writing!

Upon graduating, I published parts of my dissertation in professional journals. With degrees under my belt, I steered my educational pursuits in two directions. First, I joined Toastmaster's International to learn public speaking. In 1989, I published the first of about a dozen articles in *The Toastmaster*, actually getting paid for a few. Second, I enrolled in the American Hypnosis Training Academy, directed by Ron Klein, in Silver Spring, Maryland. I spent the next five years in training (while working a full-time job) to acquire advanced certifications in clinical hypnotherapy and NLP.

I became absolutely intrigued with the ways in which communication influences thinking and behavior. That's why, in 1992, even though I was working as a project manager for a Department of Defense contracting firm, I started a part-time, solo counseling/coaching practice. I left corporate work in 2004 to practice full time.

In 1992, I also became an associate trainer with Ron: a masterful storyteller, methodical trainer, and superbly sensitive NLP practitioner/trainer. I taught with him for over a decade, learning about stage presence and rapport. I learned how to teach and demonstrate NLP processes. Today, Ron and I continue to collaborate as directors of the National Board for Certified Clinical Hypnotherapists. In 1997, I began publishing book reviews and articles on NLP and hypnotherapy.

I wanted to write books, but I wasn't sure I knew enough about anything to fill even a slender volume. Sometimes I sat down to write and nothing happened. Or, more likely, what occurred was so bad I threw it away. Once more, fate stepped in.

In 1999, while I was teaching an NLP course, a student named Kathy Corsetty invited me to co-author a book with her. Kathy is a remarkable person. Sometime before we met, she attended a Tony Robbins seminar. Inspired by his NLP-based approach to personal mastery, she learned all she could about nutrition and exercise, dropped 40 pounds, and competed in a triathlon. She wanted to relate her experience in a book. As co-author, I would explain how NLP fosters behavioral change. In 2000, Kathy self-published *Healthy Habits* and we eventually sold a few copies. Some remain in a box in my hallway closet.

A few overweight clients enlisted my services because they liked what they read in *Healthy Habits*. Through trial and error, I eventually developed an eight-session, hypnotherapy and NLP-based weight reduction program. During that time, I was leading a monthly NLP practitioner discussion group. I taught the program to participants. One said, "You ought to write a book about this!" I spent the next year working on a manuscript. In 2005, I submitted a book proposal to Crown House Publishing

I chose Crown House because, to them, I believe I was something of a known quantity. I landed on their reviewers' list in 1997 when I reviewed *The Spirit of NLP* by L. Michael Hall (1995) for *Anchor Point* magazine. I figured if any publisher would give me a chance, it would be Crown House. *The Weight, Hypnotherapy, and You Weight Reduction Program* reached publication in 2006. A second book, *Why Do I Keep Doing This!!?* was published in 2012.

I have joined that strange breed of people unable resist the urge to put fingertips to the keyboard, despite wastebaskets full of jettisoned drafts, little hope of financial remuneration, and the ever-present possibility of rejection.

I give you my credentials with humility. Even in the narrow niche of NLP authors, I'm small potatoes compared to those who have achieved international acclaim. Even though I regard myself as a beginning writer with much to learn, I can attest that NLP has been a huge help. That's what I want to share with you.

NLP Enriches the Writing Process

Somewhere along the way to getting published, I started applying NLP to my writing. NLP communication patterns helped me write more clearly. When I applied NLP to the *task* of writing, my productivity improved. I caught my clumsiness more easily. I became more patient in working out glitches and inconsistencies (my editors and proofreaders might disagree). I became more open to criticism. I got better at switching perspectives between writer and reader; writer and editor. Soon I was coaching other new authors in NLP.

I wondered: had anyone ever written a book about how NLP improves writing? Surely, I thought, I couldn't be the only one who knew this! Many NLP trainers have written about NLP applications, ranging from teambuilding to stuttering. Despite all the books about NLP, I found only one that discussed how to apply NLP to writing. That book was *The POWER Process: An NLP Approach to Writing* published in 1997 by Dixie Elise Hickman and Sid Jacobson.

The POWER Process guides the reader, work-book style, through a writing project. It discusses the unique requirements of various types of projects. The case studies are instructive and the book discusses how to beat writer's block. I like the book and have found it helpful in my own projects. Nevertheless, I thought I could add something to the discussion, building on Hickman and Jacobson's fine work.

Improve Your Writing with NLP percolated in the recesses of my mind for about three years before I could free up my schedule to pound on it in earnest. Now, I intend to tell you how NLP can make *your* writing process more rewarding and, perhaps, less daunting.

I will not tell you how to get published or how to market your work. Books on these topics abound. The annual tome, *Writer's Market* (2012), is a goldmine of such information. You'll find it in the reference room of your public library.

I will not discuss the mechanics of grammar, sentence structure, composition, and style. For these, there is no equal to Strunk and White's *The Elements of Style* (1999). If you don't own it, get it. Read it.

This book is about NLP's unique contribution to the *process* of writing, from nurturing your tiny seed of an idea to getting feedback on your finished manuscript. It's about how NLP strategies can help you to access your creativity, hone your craft, and evaluate your work. It's about how NLP communication patterns can help you varnish what you say when you arrange words on a page.

What is NLP?

You might say NLP is a method for deciphering the operations of the human mind. NLP is useful to writers in three ways: it's a way to model excellence, solve problems, and improve communication.

- **Modeling excellence:** If we can figure out how people organize their thoughts to arrive at a particular result, then we can organize our own thoughts in a similar manner to get a similar result. That "figuring out" is called modeling. NLP is an approach to modeling behavior change and performance excellence.

- **Problem-solving:** If we can observe and understand how people organize their thoughts when faced with a problem, then we can teach them how to get a better result—a solution. With NLP strategies, you can solve self-imposed problems that have gotten in the way of your best writing.

- **Communication:** NLP is the study of excellence in human communication, verbal and non-verbal, interpersonal and intrapersonal.

NLP helps with organizing your work, managing your mindset, and communicating effectively. Now about the term: Neuro-Linguistic Programming. You might be wondering what it means. So let me simplify it.

Neuro refers to the human neurological system with which we process information in such a way as to experience cognition, emotions, and physical responses that generate behaviors.

Linguistic refers to the fact that we translate all perceived experience into some form of communication that holds meaning and implications. Thus, we have a continual and reciprocal interplay between experience and our interpretations and representations of that experience.

Programming refers to how we sequence and organize our neurological processes (thoughts, ideas, self-talk, etc.) to arrive at specific behavioral and emotional outcomes.

Richard Bandler, John Grinder and other developers of NLP originally characterized the human neurological system as something similar to a computer system. The input is the information that comes in via our senses. The output consists of behaviors, emotions, and physical responses. The software with which we program our neurological systems consists of our internal representations and our strategies for processing information (i.e. decision-making, problem-solving, and so on). If we don't like the results we're getting, it's time to modify the programming. NLP provides the tools and methods for doing so.

NLP is about Mental Strategies—Mindsets

When a cognitive process typically follows a particular sequence of perceptions and internal representations, the sequence is then called, in NLP terminology, a strategy. You know a person is running a strategy when you hear something like this: "When my boss walked into my office, I said to myself, 'Uh oh.' I pictured his angry look when my report was late yesterday. I remembered the critical tone in his voice. I immediately felt nervous. My stomach felt queasy."

We run strategies all the time, unconsciously. Good spellers use one strategy and poor spellers use another. A writer who gets ill-tempered under a tight deadline uses a different strategy from someone who simply pours forth more effort and concentration. NLP makes strategies evident. When we know the steps in problematic strategies, then we can experiment with changing the various steps to arrive at new outcomes.

Our strategies are derived from visual, auditory, kinesthetic, gustatory, and olfactory input to the brain. Internally, we "re-present" experience through these same five sensory "modalities." On an *objective* level, our internal experience is the result of neuro-chemical events. On a *subjective* level, we think in pictures and words. Meaning is based on a web of memories and associations. The meanings of our internal representations generate emotions and physical sensations. Some of our visual and auditory representations are remembered (via memory); some are constructed (via imagination).

Anchoring: Change Your Behavior by Changing Your Mindset

Anchoring is NLP's predominant behavioral-change strategy. It's a means to access a resourceful state. "State" refers to one's mind-and-body condition at any given moment. A state is systemic, involving thinking, emotions, sensations, and behaviors.

A "resourceful" state is one appropriate to a given circumstance. Unresourceful states are problematic to a given circumstance. Confidence is a good state for a job interview. Nervousness isn't.

We usually name states by the emotions we feel: happy, sad, excited, angry, motivated, and so on. Sometimes we name states depending on how we perceive others behave toward us. Thus, we can *feel* appreciated, loved, insulted, ignored, and so on. Sometimes we name states according to our physical condition: feverish, nauseated, sleepy, tired, alert, energetic, and so on.

Anchoring is based on classical conditioning; what Pavlov did with his dogs. Dogs naturally salivate when they get meat—especially if they are hungry. Pavlov presented his hungry dogs with meat, pairing each presentation with the ringing of a bell. Eventually, through association, the dogs learned to salivate at the ringing of the bell alone. Anchoring is this kind of associative learning.

The NLP literature has many variations on anchoring. Here is a generic template:

1. Identify a type of situation in which you've generally felt unresourceful. By this, I mean that you've usually responded to that particular situation or context in a manner that you dislike—you get into a problematic state.

2. Think of a specific instance of that situation. Review what happened. Notice the trigger that activated your unresourceful response (something you saw, heard, felt, or thought about). You are describing the first step of your problematic strategy. You'll replace that strategy with a different one that leads to a better outcome.

3. Ask yourself, "What resourceful state would I need to handle that situation more effectively?" A resourceful state is one that you're pretty sure will bring about a better outcome.

4. Identify an unrelated situation (a different context from the problematic one) in which you reliably access the resourceful state you

identified in Step 3. In NLP, we call this second circumstance the "solution" context.

5. Remember a specific instance in which you accessed your resourceful state in the solution context. Pretend you've stepped back into the moment, remembering the sights, sounds, smells, tastes, and sensations. Imagine you are there right now. Take time with this step and you'll automatically access that resourceful state.

6. Pair your resourceful state with a distinct cue (anchor) that you can control (a specific word or a tactile sensation, such as squeezing two fingers together).

7. Repeat steps 5 and 6 three to five times to condition the response.

8. Return your thoughts to the here-and-now, allowing the resourceful state feelings to linger.

9. Imagine the next time you'll encounter the type of situation that was problematic (the situation you identified in Step 1). Pretend you are there right now—in a future situation. This time, you'll have a different response. Apply your cue immediately when you first notice the triggering event. Instantly access your resourceful state, thinking quality thoughts and feeling resourceful emotions. Play out the scenario with new thoughts, feelings, and actions. Notice the improvements in your feelings and possibly your actions. This step, by the way, is called "mental rehearsal" in psychological literature.

10. Return your thoughts to the here-and-now. Continue to occasionally think about that future circumstance where it will be useful to access your resourceful state. Mentally practice accessing your resourceful state, in that circumstance, tweaking your response until it feels familiar and comfortable.

Don't worry if anchoring seems cumbersome or complex at this point. I mainly want you to understand that NLP strategies, such as anchoring, are highly structured. Thus, they generally appear in this book as a series of numbered steps, as in the template above.

Learning a strategy in this way eliminates guesswork. You'll encounter templates for strategies throughout this book. When you do, I hope that, instead of just reading through the template, you'll actually pause and perform each step, applying the strategy to your situation.

NLP Principles for Writing

NLP rests on principles (often called "presuppositions") that make for effective communication and optimal performance. Here are ten NLP principles that apply to writing. Don't regard them as rules chiseled in stone, but instead as useful guidelines that might give you a few new ideas about writing and insights into your own behaviors as a writer. If a particular principle doesn't work for you in a given situation, disregard it.

1. **Experience has structure.** Change the structure and you change the result. This is the rationale behind NLP behavioral change strategies. Human beings tend to feel comfortable with the predictable and familiar. Therefore, we structure our actions around repetition and pattern. We develop habits.

   Sometimes we develop habits we don't want. Some unwanted habits become so deeply engrained, they function automatically. They are difficult to break. Sometimes doing one thing differently interrupts an existing pattern and establishes a new one. In NLP, altering an existing habit is called a "pattern interruption." You'll encounter that term in Chapter 1.

   Because experience has structure, it is possible to model another person's behaviors and to replicate their desirable habits in ourselves. In Chapters 2 and 3, you'll learn two models that structure the process of writing: the POWER Process and the Disney Creativity Model.

2. **Your state determines your effectiveness.** We accomplish our best results when we are in the right "state" of mind, body, and spirit. If you bound out of bed every morning feeling motivated and ready to eagerly focus your attention, you have the perfect state for writing. The rest of us slug-a-beds may struggle a bit. We might

get into a more resourceful state by going to bed earlier, passing up the 10 o'clock news or that evening martini. When we get up, we might need to brew a pot of coffee or have a brisk walk before settling down to write. In Chapters 4 through 9, you'll learn about optimum states for the various phases of the writing process.

3. **Every problematic behavior is motivated by a positive intent.** We all do things we find inappropriate or stupid and then wonder why. It's often because we are trying, unconsciously, to fulfill a positive intention—an underlying need or desire. History and biography are replete with complex individuals who made massive blunders based on good intentions. The road to hell is ... well, you know the rest. When we let our positive intentions rise to awareness, we can temper them or satisfy them in appropriate ways. You'll learn more about this in Chapter 5; a chapter on blasting through writer's block.

4. **Failure is feedback.** Failure doesn't mean you're a dolt, or you should give up, or you'll never succeed. It means you achieved an outcome different from the one you intended. Both success and failure leave a trail of clues as to how we reach outcomes. Failure holds worthwhile information. You'll learn more about resourceful responses to the possibility of failure in Chapter 5.

5. **The meaning of your communication is the response you get.** No doubt, you write to evoke a response in others, do you not? You hope that your publisher will accept your proposal; your supervisor will look favorably on your report; your instructor will bless your term paper. You might be writing to teach, inform, entertain, inspire, or persuade. You hope your readers will respond accordingly.

   If they don't, it's easy to blame *them* for not recognizing your brilliance. Nevertheless, this NLP principle suggests that you work very hard on matching your communication to the characteristics, needs, and expectations of your readers. You'll learn more about how to do this in Chapter 7.

6. **The map is not the territory.** This statement originated with Alfred Korzybski, the father of modern linguistics. It means our thoughts and understandings are not reality; they *represent* reality. Our internal "maps" contain three types of limitations:

    - Deletions: Some information is omitted.
    - Distortions: Some information is ambiguous.
    - Generalizations: Some information is exaggerated or applied to contexts where it is inappropriate.

    Deletions, distortions, and generalizations can sometimes make our ideas seem vague and our writing confusing. That's when the NLP Meta Model proves helpful. It's a method for detecting and correcting deletions, distortions, and generalizations. The result is increased clarity and specificity. You'll learn more about the Meta Model in Chapter 8 and in Appendix B.

7. **Humans learn by making mistakes.** Mistakes are a great source of information. Editors take delight in finding them. You should too. Through catching and correcting mistakes, you'll sharpen your skills. We don't always notice our own mistakes. That's why it's so essential to be open to feedback and criticism (see Chapter 9 for more information).

8. **If something is difficult, chunk it down into smaller steps.** Just as you would eat a watermelon one bite at a time, you'll want to break large projects into manageable chunks. If you are writing a book, for instance, you could write for an hour each day, or strive for a certain number of words each day. You'll learn more about chunking down large projects in Chapter 11.

9. **People have all the internal resources they need.** This optimistic assumption says that no one is a hopeless case. We all have the ability to learn, improve, recover from setbacks, adapt to change, and accomplish goals, provided we have the right strategies. Granted, many people possess what the world regards as disadvantages. But many such people have astounded the world with what they do. Look around and you'll see remarkable people doing things many of us would have said were impossible.

For you, this principle means that you have the ability to achieve what you want to as a writer. Getting there may be a matter of developing your talents, managing your time, learning the business end of writing, and so on. Success is reliably difficult, but doable in the long run.

These principles have weathered the test of time and are just as relevant today as when they first appeared in NLP training courses over 40 years ago. Choose one or two that speak to you and keep them in mind for your current project. It might give you satisfaction that you now know more about NLP than probably 99% of the world's writers.

The NLP Success Formula—for Writing

Although it started over 40 years ago, NLP has not faded into history. In fact, it is flourishing worldwide.

NLP began as an adjunct to psychotherapy: it was based on studying the communication patterns of three pioneering psychotherapists of the 1970s, the most prominent of whom was Milton H. Erickson, M.D. (1901–1980). The other two were Fritz Perls (1893–1970) and Virginia Satir (1916–1988). Today, NLP has applications in education, life coaching, motivational training, business management and consulting, sales and marketing, and sports psychology. NLP shows up in thousands of books and training programs in many languages. The Association of NLP, headquartered in London, holds an annual conference that draws speakers from around the globe.

My intent in this book is to translate NLP into practical advice that you can implement at each stage of the writing process to increase productivity and give new dimensions to your content. Here is the basic NLP Success Formula, applied to writing:

1. **Know your outcome.** When you begin a project, ask: What will I write about? What is my purpose? Who is my typical reader? How can I engage my reader? Where can I find the information I need? Formulate an idea of your finished product to the extent that you can describe it.

2. **Take action.** Develop a plan and act on it. Organize your work schedule. Outline the content. Do the research. Put your fingers on the keyboard and make words, sentences, and paragraphs appear.

3. **Determine whether you are getting your outcome.** Periodically, pause to evaluate. Is your content moving in the right direction? Are you staying on message? Is the style consistent? Are you following the outline? Is the project on schedule? Keep evaluating your progress.

4. **Alter your behavior if you aren't getting your outcome.** If you see that your product isn't matching your expectations, modify your approach. You might need to revise your outline or do more research. Maybe you need to extend your deadline or modify your schedule. Keep revising your process and your product until both meet with your satisfaction. Get feedback from others as well.

5. **Operate from a state of excellence.** No one writes well when feeling tired, sick, intoxicated, distracted, or stressed. Take care of yourself physically, emotionally, mentally, and spiritually so that you have the energy to excel.

In the pages that follow, you'll operationalize the NLP Success Formula. In Chapter 1, you'll encounter the NLP concept called Logical Levels: this concept will invite you to examine the meaning of what it is to be a writer in all respects. In Chapters 2 and 3 you'll learn two overlapping and complementary models for writing excellence: the POWER Process and the Disney Creativity Model. The POWER Process organizes the tasks of writing into discrete steps. The Disney Creativity Model describes the three states that best accommodate each phase in the process of writing.

In Chapters 4 through 9, you'll learn techniques, tips, and NLP strategies to blend these two models into your writing. Appendix A contains worksheets that will help you to apply the information in each chapter (except Chapter 11). You can, in fact, use chapters 4 through 9, and the accompanying worksheets, as a guide for your current writing project, from start to finish. If you'd like to try your hand at writing hypnotically, read Chapter 10. If you want to write prolifically, read Chapter 11.

You don't need certification in NLP to understand this book. Put simply, NLP explains what people do when they are at their best. Chances are that you are already using NLP principles, strategies, and communication patterns, at times, without even realizing it. My hope is that NLP will bring out your best writing.

CHAPTER 1

How Does it *Feel* to *Be* a Writer?

"Writing wakes us up in a marvelous way. It forces us to notice, to see, to hear, to feel, to develop sensory awareness ... Writing gently invites us to become more authentic, more known to ourselves."

L. Michael Hall

The imposter syndrome is a strange quirk of human psychology. It happens when people acquire the trappings of success, but they don't *feel* successful. Among their peers and colleagues, they feel like an interloper—someone who doesn't belong. Sometimes they worry that they will somehow be exposed as a phony or that others will reject them. A silent question hovers behind each accomplishment: What if I'm not good enough?

We'll never know how much talent and ingenuity the world has been denied because of the imposter syndrome. We'll never know how many people have stalled out in their careers or shrunk their aspirations because of thinking they are "not good enough".

Do you feel comfortable in thinking of yourself as a writer? Maybe you worry that others will deride your ambitions. Maybe you think your skills will just never match those of the really great writers in your genre. Perhaps you think no one will ever care about what you write about anything. If you've been thinking small about your potential, this chapter is for you.

To congruently accomplish your goals as a writer, it will help if you have something to write about, possess sufficient skill, believe in your abilities, establish a writer's felt identity, and perceive a purpose in your writing. The NLP Logical Levels will guide you in developing a consistency and continuity of experience so that you embrace the writer's role on your own terms.

The Logical Levels concept was developed by NLP trainer Robert Dilts, (Dilts and DeLozier, 2000), who was inspired by the English anthropologist, Gregory Bateson (1904–1980). The concept is a modeling tool for understanding the salient, subjective aspects of any given human process. By eliciting strategies (see the Introduction) and asking questions about Logical Levels, it's possible to understand and model a specific outcome—in this case, developing your identity as a writer.

The NLP Logical Levels form a six-level hierarchy. Each level seeks to answer specific questions. For writers, these levels are:

1. **Environment:** Where? Where you do most of your writing.

2. **Behaviors:** What? The behaviors that constitute your writing.

3. **Capabilities:** How? The knowledge and skills that you bring to your writing.

4. **Beliefs and Values:** Why? The values and beliefs behind your writing.

5. **Identity:** Who? The roles you take on in the various tasks of writing.

6. **Spirituality:** Meaning: Connecting your writing to a meaningful purpose. Doing so necessitates that you share your message with others.

When people encounter a difficulty in adapting or learning a new behavior, we can often detect where the problem lies by asking about each level:

- Does the environment allow and support this new behavior?

- Does the individual know what to do?

- Does the individual possess the needed knowledge, skills, strategies, and tools?

- Do the individual's values and beliefs allow him or her to feel congruent in this behavior?

- Does this individual's identity match the requirements of the behavior?

- How does this behavior affect the individual's relationship with a larger purpose or ideal?

In theory, the Logical Levels are systemic, meaning that change at one level affects processes and outcomes at other levels. The levels are also hierarchical. People are likely to change behavior when the environment supports that change and when they know what to do and how to do it. Nevertheless, they will resist change if it contradicts their beliefs and values, their identity, or their spiritual ideals.

Logical Levels can be applied not only as a way to understand (model) a process or behavior, and to determine the level at which behavioral problems occur, but also to influence behavior. In this chapter, we'll examine each Logical Level in the life of a writer. The Chapter 1 worksheet (in Appendix A) contains an action item for each level.

Environment: Where You Write

Professional writers usually have an office, study, or cubbyhole where they go to write undisturbed. They shut the door. They make the environment conducive to their work, considering noise levels, lighting, supplies, furnishings, and amenities; say, for example, a coffeemaker. Reference materials are within easy reach. A comfortable environment promotes concentration and productivity.

Equipment and tools are also an essential part of a writer's environment. Do you have what you need? With technology advancing and changing so rapidly, it's a good idea to ensure that your computer equipment, peripherals, and software are suitable for your needs—and possibly for the format requirements of your publisher, faculty, workplace, or clients.

If you travel frequently, your writing environment might include airports, trains, planes, diners, coffee-shops, and hotel rooms. Forgoing the luxury of a private little nook, you'll want the equipment and technological gadgets that make for portability. Laptops, computer notebooks, audio pocket recorders, smart-phones, jump drives, and Wi-Fi connections are a boon to writers on the go!

Behavior: What You Do

Professional writers organize their projects and schedule writing time. They organize content around a central idea, purpose, or requirement. They outline. They check references and do research. They consult experts. They get feedback. They revise and fact-check. They verify that they've met contract specifications and format requirements. This is the production side of writing.

There's also the business end of writing to consider. Successful freelancers understand their business demands all too well. A writer-for-hire, a copywriter for instance, markets writing services, often to clientele in a specific industry. They assemble a marketing kit and a website showing work samples and testimonials from satisfied clients. They develop a mailing list and follow up on leads. They attend conferences and join professional associations to network and keep tabs on their industry. They establish themselves as experts through publishing articles and books, and giving speeches and seminars. They set their fees, write proposals, and bid on contracts.

Many authors don't knuckle down to produce serious content until they have a contract (and if they are *really* successful, a cash advance) in hand. Getting that contract may require selecting a magazine editor or book publisher, sending a query, and/or writing a proposal. Established authors who write many books, screen plays, and articles in a competitive genre, such as romance or science fiction, hire an agent to promote their work and negotiate contracts with publishers.

If you self-publish a book, you'll manage (and/or outsource) every aspect of production, formatting, selecting a publishing platform, pricing, printing, and distribution. You'll be solely responsible for marketing the book through email campaigns, writing a blog, sending it to reviewers, getting it into bookstores, promoting it on a website, and getting it into online stores, such as Amazon.

If you write an e-book, you can market it through a blog, newsletter, or website, or through an e-book website, such as Smashwords or Kindle Direct Publishing, that will handle the distribution for you.

Some writers work in a salaried position as a journalist, speechwriter, editor, marketer, copywriter, or proposal writer. If you want employment as a *salaried* writer, build a diversified portfolio of published, relevant work. Maintain a list of your publications. Create a résumé that highlights your writing experience. When you apply for a job, send your résumé and a sample of your work. Collect solid letters of reference from people who praise your writing as well as your knowledge of your topic and industry. Know and use the terminology of your industry. Make your cover letters professional, yet uniquely demonstrative of your skills; not just tooting your horn, but focusing on the needs of the prospective employer.

See your writing career as a progression of levels of accomplishment. Many authors start writing as a hobby or part-time self-employment for extra income. Some use their writing as a sideline to excel in a profession where excellent communication skills are essential to advancement. Some use writing to launch a career as a speaker, consultant, trainer, or media personality.

Capability: Your Know-how

Now that you know *what* to do, are you sure you have the skills and knowledge to do it? Are you satisfied with your writing skills? Are you satisfied with your business skills?

Reading is the best way to improve your skills in creating content. Reading is the creative center of a writer's life. Subscribe to journals, magazines, blogs, and newsletters in your genre. Read works by other authors. Learn to discriminate good writing from the mediocre. Measure your own skills against the good and the great. Start to recognize various styles. Notice what has been done and what hasn't, what is trite and what's fresh (King, 2000).

Read works by the best authors in your genre and model their standards. Read everything you can by them and about them. Read what others say about their work. If your favorite authors are current-day figures, follow their blogs, subscribe to their newsletters, and attend their classes or speaking engagements.

When one of your favorite authors publishes a new book, review it. If nothing else, post the review on your own blog or with an online bookseller, such as Amazon. Reviewing other's books will improve your absorption of content as well as your recognition of variations in style. In academic writing, you'll see where each writer's contribution conforms to or contradicts the body of knowledge in the subject matter. By subscribing to magazines, journals, blogs, and newsletters, you'll know which ones solicit reviews. By blogging, reviewing, and commenting astutely on works in your sphere of expertise, you'll eventually be regarded as a "thought leader" in your field.

Many fledgling writers benefit enormously from hiring a writing coach. A coach can give you one-on-one help in formulating realistic goals, examining your blockages, evaluating options, and figuring out solutions. He or she will help you stay on track and get past sticking points, serving as a confidante, mentor, and sounding board. If you need help developing a plan and maintaining a work schedule, your coach will gladly hold you accountable for your commitments.

I suggest you collect books and articles about your subject matter or genre, and about writing and publishing. I have shelves of books on communication, NLP and hypnotherapy, as well as a filing cabinet of articles and workshop handouts, and several e-books downloaded to my laptop computer. My home library also has a reference section with books on writing style and composition, and how to get published. So much to read, so little time!

When it comes to skill improvement, my biggest challenge has been keeping up with advances in information technologies that are creating new media for distribution as well as marketing. I've learned how to create e-books and write a blog. I've had fun learning to work in a recording studio with an audio technician to produce commercial audio recordings (hypnosis CDs and downloads). I'm learning to share information through webinars, teleconferences, and email newsletters.

Professional writers outsource many tasks that they don't know how to do or don't want to do. You can outsource illustrations and graphic design, website design, copyediting, transcribing, and e-book formatting. Where do you find such services? Start with www.elance.com, www.freelance.com, www.odesk.com or www.guru.com. You can also hire companies to obtain your permissions and ensure that your work doesn't violate any registered trademarks or copyrights.

Beliefs that Support Success

Beliefs exert powerful influence over decisions, actions, and emotions. They filter our perceptions. They shape our values about what's fair, honest, ethical, moral, true, possible, and worthwhile. They are the scaffolding on which we hang our hopes and ambitions.

Successful and prolific writers believe in themselves. They believe they have something worthwhile to say and are willing to say it. They believe in their capabilities, even while striving for improvement. They formulate goals and believe it's possible to achieve them. Do you hold these beliefs?

If you don't believe you have what it takes, another, contrary belief might be getting in the way. In NLP, we don't judge a belief by whether it is true or false, but by how well it serves our purposes. Limiting beliefs impede mastery and accomplishment. They are like dragons that stalk our intentions and diminish our hopes. Dragon beliefs show up in the disparaging things we tell ourselves. Here are a few examples:

> I could never be that good.
> No one would want to read this.
> I'm too old. I should have started years ago.
> I'm too young. I have no credibility.

I'll probably make a fool of myself.
I'm getting nowhere—I should just quit.
There's too much competition.

The good news is that you can replace dragon beliefs with empowering beliefs that instill confidence and persistence and improve your problem-solving skills. Later in this chapter, and in Chapter 5, you'll read about some ways to shake up dragon beliefs

Identity: Step into the Writer's Role

Identity is a guiding concept of who you are, made up of the roles you fill in life: parent, child, sibling, citizen, male or female, employer or employee, and so on. Roles surface and submerge according to context (environment) and the stages of life. Each role requires specific capabilities and carries with it a complex system of beliefs, expectations, and responsibilities that shape behavior.

How do you feel about your identity (role) as a writer? Do you feel comfy or awkward and tentative, like an imposter? The more experience you acquire, the more congruent you'll feel in saying, "I'm a writer." Taking on a writer's identity includes developing your style and expertise while targeting your readership.

Your identity as a writer requires that you produce something for people to read. You acquire the know-how to post articles, blog, submit queries and proposals, self-publish, or fulfill assignments. If you are a novice, getting your work before the eyes of others might be a daunting process. It means people will scrutinize your work, form opinions about it, and comment on it or critique it. Rejection and criticism come with the territory. Don't let either deter you from your path or diminish your identity. Keep writing and improving.

The more completely you immerse yourself in the world of writers and writing, the more competent you'll feel. Get involved with other writers.

How? Participate in a writer's guild. Attend book fairs and trade shows where your favorite authors are speaking or signing books. Carry your portfolio and business cards to writer's conferences and networking events. Serendipity happens when people with similar interests meet to share ideas, news, and business leads.

By networking, you might find the perfect co-author or someone to write the foreword to your next book. You might meet the editor of a magazine who is looking for the article that only you can write! At trade shows, you can meet publishing company representatives and find out if your subject matter is a good match for their market. When you let people know what you write about, your name might come up when someone is looking for a specialty piece such as a topical article, case study, short story, or a chapter in a compilation.

Collaborating with other writers will enlarge your identity as a writer. Here are a few ways to collaborate:

- Interview your favorite author for a magazine or newsletter in your field.

- Co-lead a seminar or workshop with an author whose work complements yours.

- Sit on a panel discussion at a professional conference.

- Ask other authors to contribute a chapter or a case study to your book.

- If you self-publish, ask other authors for a pre-publication review or endorsement of your book. If you have a book contract, your publisher will take care of this step. You can, however, supply names of potential reviewers.

- If you know a local author in your genre who makes speaking appearances, recommend him or her as a guest speaker for your professional organization or corporate meeting. Even though an official may make the arrangements regarding the speaking contract and payment, you could still volunteer to escort the speaker and serve as his or her assistant for the day.

- Co-author a book, article, or information product.

- If you are qualified to do so, teach a class on some aspect of writing or publishing. Find a venue through your local adult education office. You might inspire a future author who will want to collaborate with *you*!

- Ask a fellow author to promote your information product in his or her newsletter or blog (and arrange an affiliate commission).

In any joint venture where payments and royalties are involved, make sure you and your collaborator have agreement as to how you will share the responsibilities and proceeds.

By interacting with other authors, especially those in your genre, your topic, and possibly your industry, you will benefit from exchanging information, knowledge, and mutual support. You will get to know and learn from others who share your identity. You will realize you belong.

Spirituality: Share Your Message

Your writing will take on a more intense meaning and personal significance when it makes a contribution, supports a cause, or satisfies a need. Yes, writers write for personal gain—for the money, the promotion, the contract, or the recognition. They won't get those rewards, however, until their writing somehow meets others' needs, desires, and expectations. When you write for the benefit of your readers (or your clients and/or customers) as well as your own, you acquire an additional dimension of awareness and sensory acuity.

The most successful writers strive to enrich the lives of others and better the world around them. Successful writers derive pleasure when they inform, entertain, inspire, persuade, and move people to action. They believe in the value of what they produce and consider writing as a means to answer a calling. They feel excitement about their content and their readers. They are dedicated to the craft and the beauty of words. The spiritual dimensions of writing make people feel passionate about doing it!

What do You Believe?

What do you currently believe about your potential as a writer? What is your ultimate goal as a writer? Come on, be expansive! What do you really want? A bestseller? A movie contract? A Pulitzer? A six-figure income? University tenure? As you formulate that goal, notice what's going on in your head. Listen to the inner conversation. What do you hear?

Empowering beliefs shape the thinking and actions that make for success. Does your inner dialog support your goal and bestow confidence in your abilities? If you hear doubt and discouragement, translate that feeling into a statement that reveals a dragon belief. Write down that belief and examine it. This limiting belief says you can't have what you want. You can neutralize that belief.

Below are four simple tactics to dismantle a limiting belief and make it seem silly (Andreas, 2012). These "pattern interruptions" alter the look, sound, and feel of a belief statement. As you experiment with each one, focus your awareness inward. Notice changes that occur in your thoughts and emotions that diminish the feelings of certainty around that dragon belief.

- **Change the sound of the words.** Listen to the voice in your head that expresses the belief. Make it speak faster. Make it speak slower. Make it into a hoarse whisper. Make it sound like Mickey Mouse or Donald Duck.

- **Change the location of the voice.** Put it outside of your head by a few centimeters. Move it to the left of your head. Move it to the right of your head. Make it sound as though it is coming from the next room.

- **Change the physical sensations.** Say the belief statement aloud in a silly voice while hopping on one foot (or making any unusual, playful movement).

- **See the words in a new way.** With your non-dominant hand, write the belief on a page of paper. With a crayon, write it backwards. Write each word on a sticky note. Put the notes on a wall, spaced about an arm's length apart. Change the order of the notes until the statement is nonsensical.

As you perform these exercises, you'll probably notice that the belief statement is losing credibility because you are representing it in a new way and creating new associations.

The final step is to formulate a replacement belief. What would you rather believe? What would you *have to* believe in order to reach your goals? Write it down. Put it where you can see it. Repeat it until it feels comfortable and familiar.

How Will You Know?

NLP practitioners often ask "How will you know?" It's a request for evidence-based criteria. If you aspire to be a writer and want to *feel* congruent in that identity, then how will you *know* when that happens? What will constitute your evidence? One way to answer the question is to model other accomplished writers.

I highly esteem L. Michael Hall, one of the most innovative trainers and authors in NLP. In 2001, he wrote an article in *Anchor Point* titled, "Games Prolific Writers Play". In it, he described his passion for writing, providing a window into the mind, heart, and soul of a writer. No imposter syndrome here!

Hall writes to learn—to burrow into his subject matter and discover it not only from his own perspective and experience, but also from the perspectives of other authors. He writes first for himself—to capture his own understandings, insights, and opinions—before deciding whether and how to share them with others.

Then he got to the core of how it feels: "... I cannot not write. I find it so pleasurable that if it became illegal and a felony ... I'd go underground to write. To play with ideas, to find new ways to express a thrilling understanding, to explore what I don't know, and find out what I do—these are the psychic and semantic pleasures of writing." (p. 25)

Ahh! So *that's* how it feels to be a writer!

CHAPTER 2

Get Organized with the POWER Process Model

"We could probably create a new model of the writing process for each writer, each one slightly different; there is no ONE WAY that must be followed. Yet there are certain basic patterns every successful writer follows."

Dixie Elise Hickman and Sid Jacobson

When you read a book, an article, or a research paper, or when you see a play, a movie, or documentary, you see a writer's finished product. As with any finished product, you really don't see all the work that went into it. Good writing makes the finished product flow effortlessly, word by word, moment by moment. Effective writing is about what happens *before* publication—the process of developing, organizing, researching, and communicating ideas.

When we can elicit or determine another's strategies and understand the Logical Levels of his or her experience, we can then develop a model of how that individual gets a particular outcome. In this chapter, I'll explain one of two NLP models for excellence in writing: the POWER Process model, developed by Dixie Elise Hickman and Sid Jacobson (1997). In the next chapter, I'll explain the other model, the Disney Creativity Model, developed by Robert Dilts (1994).

The two models overlap. While the POWER Process examines the *mechanics* of writing, the Disney Creativity Model examines the *mindsets* that make for good writing at each stage of the process. These two models lay a foundation for Chapters 4 through 9.

Dixie Elise Hickman is an educator and writing/editing consultant trained in NLP. Sid Jacobson is an author and NLP trainer. Together, they developed the POWER Process and tested it by analyzing common activities of successful writers. Next, they compared successful writers' patterns with those of people who had trouble writing, finding specific differences. They then taught the successful patterns to people who had trouble writing and found that these people improved.

The POWER Process (an acronym) consists of five steps—Previewing, Organizing, Writing, Evaluating, and Revising—as explained throughout the remainder of this chapter.

Previewing

Think of previewing as preliminary planning. When you perform this step well, the other four steps in the process flow smoothly. Previewing has five components, explained below, with the acronym, SPACE:

- **Self:** The first consideration is how to present yourself—to define your identity in communicating your message to the reader. How do you want to come across? What role do you take as the author? You might, for instance, write an academic paper as a researcher. You might write a self-help book as an expert advisor. The role you choose will set the tone of your writing.

- **Purpose:** The next consideration is your purpose or interrelated purposes. What do you want to accomplish with your project? What do you want to happen for those who read your work? Your purpose determines your scope to some extent. Define your purpose and your writing will be more consistent throughout, with no rambling into the irrelevant.

- **Audience:** Who are your readers? Determine what your readers want from you. Decide the criteria by which they will judge your finished product. By identifying your audience in advance, you'll better determine how to make your purpose compatible with your readers' needs, expectations, and criteria. Chapter 7 has more information about writing for your readers.

- **Code:** Code is the means by which you communicate your message and the manner in which you present your information. Code refers to your genre. It governs your choice of vocabulary, layout, illustrations, and examples. For a scholarly work, you'll want to consult published author guidelines and style guides, as appropriate. Code also refers to the final medium of your work, such as a hard copy book, magazine article, pamphlet, slide presentation, film, audio recording, speech, wall poster, or computer download.

- **Experience:** What is your experience in your topic? What background and information do you bring to the table? Perhaps you have enough information to be considered an expert, or possibly you need to acquire additional knowledge through research or training. If the information you currently possess is insufficient, your planning will include where to locate additional sources.

Previewing calls for crucial decisions that will determine the direction of the remaining four steps. Previewing creates an initial vision of your project. It helps you determine the compatibility of your role, your purpose, and your readers. It alerts you to options for presenting and communicating your message. It informs you of any need to gather additional information. Take time with this step.

Organizing

The next step is to organize your planned content so that you can present it in a logical structure. The most common method for organizing content is the outline.

The longer your manuscript, the more you need an outline to keep track of where to place each component. As you proceed to write, you may find places where the outline isn't working, and you'll revise it. You might decide to add, delete, replace, split, combine, replace, or relocate portions of the manuscript to make it coherent. You might move around entire chapters to get a more logical sequence. Nevertheless, an outline is an essential starting place for organizing your ideas and planning your work.

A formal outline uses a protocol based on Roman numerals, upper case letters, numbers, and lower case letters, in descending order, like this:

I. First Main Point
   A. First Subdivision of First Main Point
      1. First Subdivision of A
         a. First subdivision of A1
         b. Second subdivision of A1
      2. Second Subdivision of A
         a. First subdivision of A2
         b. Second subdivision of A2
   B. Second Subdivision of First Main Point

II. Second Main Point

Some people dislike formal outlines because of the complexity or formality of Roman numerals, upper case letters, lower case letters, and so forth. Unless you are submitting your outline for someone else's requirements, Roman numerals really don't matter. An informal outline can simply indent for each class of subordinate headings, like this:

Main Heading #1
   Subordinate Heading for #1
      Second order subordinate heading

Main Heading #2
   Subordinate Heading for #2
      Second order subordinate heading

Many writing specialties, such as proposals, technical reports, research studies, case studies, curriculum design, and policy manuals have their own "boilerplate" outlines. A typical research study outline, for example, might look like this:

Title
Authors
Abstract
Problem Statement
   Review of Previous Studies
   Definitions

Purpose of the Study
    Hypothesis to be Tested
Research Method
    Subjects
        Subject Selection Methods
        Subject Demographics
    Variables
    Treatment
    Measurements
    Case Example
Findings
    Methods of Analysis
    Results
Discussion/Conclusions
References

You can find these types of standard outlines in author guides and style manuals in your field. If you can't obtain a guide or style manual, look at publications and products similar to the one you want to write. Examine the way in which the content is organized and copy the commonalities.

If you have trouble generating an outline, you might want to first simply play around with your central idea and expand on it, using methods such as a mindmap or a storyboard. Read about these methods in Chapter 4.

One of the major advantages of organizing your work is to direct any necessary research. Research often fills the gap between organizing content and writing about it. Your content may require statistics, scientific findings, case studies, interviews, news stories, interviews, or quotes by experts. Research will back up your assertions with facts and add credibility to your content.

Writing

Once you've organized your content, and conducted any necessary research, begin writing your draft. Now your aim is to get something down on paper, without worrying about grammar, spelling, or elegance. You'll take care of those things later, when you revise. Let your narrative flow as spontaneously as possible, in all its imperfections, so that you'll have something to later rework. Write compulsively and impulsively!

You don't even have to start at the beginning. Just jump in where you feel most comfortable and work outward. Many writers save the introduction and the conclusion until last, to achieve consistency with the main body of the text.

If you feel intimidated by a blank page, develop ways to get your creativity flowing. Speak into a voice recorder and then transcribe your spoken words. Write to music. Go back to your outline and drill down into additional detail. You'll find more ways to surmount writer's block in Chapter 5 and ways to stay on task in Chapter 6.

Evaluating

To evaluate is to review your draft for structure, consistency, and clarity. You'll learn how to conduct a thorough, top-down analysis in Chapter 8. For now, here are the items you'll typically evaluate:

- Compare the draft to your original outline. Did you include all the central concepts and subtopics? Are there any gaps in the content? Is there anything to weed out? Does the information follow a logical sequence throughout?

- Does the narrative give you, the author, a consistent role and tone of voice?

- Does the content accomplish your original purpose? Are there places where it deviates from the purpose?

- Is your research adequate to substantiate your facts and assertions? Are your citations relevant and up-to-date with current findings in the field?

- Is the formatting consistent throughout?

- Are there any places where an example, story, illustration, or diagram could facilitate the reader's understanding?

- Take a reader's perspective. Does the content meet your needs (as a reader)? Do you understand the message? Is the purpose clear? Do you understand what the author wants you to do? You'll learn about taking the reader's perspective in Chapter 7.

Many authors submit their drafts to selected readers for evaluation, giving them a checklist of topics such as the ones in the hierarchy above. Your readers might be friends or colleagues with an interest in your subject. Corporations and research groups typically present proposals and technical reports to a review panel before "going public". Chapter 9 contains additional information about obtaining feedback.

Revising

Revising puts the final polish on your work. It involves copyediting, proofreading, and fact-checking. You might do this on your own or work with a freelance proofreader or copyeditor. Even if you have a contract with a publisher who will provide editing and revising, you'll want to give your publisher the best product you can.

The POWER Process structures each step in producing a finished draft. Yet the individual steps are open-ended, allowing for flexibility and adaptation. You can find an overview of the POWER Process model in the Chapter 2 worksheet, with a list of the chapters and worksheets associated with each step.

When you submit your finished work to a publisher, magazine editor, or any sort of evaluation board or review committee, expect that it will be edited and revised, usually making for improvement. If you've done a thorough job of previewing and organizing, you'll avoid any shocking surprises. If you've done careful research, your content will garner less skepticism and more credibility. If you've done a detailed job of evaluating and revising, you'll have a much happier copyeditor. All in all, you'll face fewer requirements to rewrite portions of the draft.

CHAPTER 3

Get the Right Mindset with the Disney Creativity Model

"The point is that creativity itself involves the synthesis of different processes or phases. The Dreamer is necessary for creativity in order to form new ideas and goals. The Realist is necessary for creativity as a means to transform ideas into concrete expressions. The Critic is necessary for creativity as a filter and a stimulus for refinement."

Robert Dilts

What if you could model the inner worlds of renowned creative geniuses, such as Einstein, Aristotle, da Vinci, Mozart, or Arthur Conan Doyle?

That is what Robert Dilts did when he wrote *Strategies of Genius* (Dilts, 1994). He gathered anecdotes, historical records, and the writings of these men. With this information, he deciphered their strategies for analysis, critical thinking, problem solving, and creativity. He then drew conclusions about their beliefs, values, behavior, goals, reasoning, identity, and capabilities.

One of Dilts' subjects was Walt Disney (1901–1966), not only a quintessential cartoon artist and storyteller, but also a businessman and entrepreneur who created a multimedia empire based on books, feature-length movies, television shows, and theme parks. Dilts wrote that the source of Disney's creative genius was his ability to explore his subject matter from three perceptual positions: the Dreamer, the Realist, and the Critic.

The Dreamer playfully uses imagination to conceive of and develop an idea (Previewing in the POWER Process). The Realist transforms the idea into reality (Organizing and Writing in the POWER Process).

The Critic evaluates the product or result and makes improvements (Evaluating and Revising in the POWER Process).

While Disney was not a writer in the usual sense of the word, the Disney Creativity Model lends itself to writing excellence. This chapter summarizes Dilts' descriptions of Disney as the Dreamer, the Realist, and the Critic. Note that each state is comprised of specific thinking patterns and cognitive processes.

The Dreamer

Dilts quotes Disney as describing his work as "a thrilling adventure, and unending voyage of discovery and exploration in the realms of color, sound, and motion" (p. 164). Disney could seize upon an idea and make it evolve, fantasizing about its potential, without hesitation or inhibition. For Disney, the Dreamer state combined visual, auditory, and kinesthetic elements.

Disney accessed the Dreamer state by going into deep thought, as though in a hypnotic trance. In Dilts' words, "The trance-like quality attributed to Disney's behavior while 'dreaming' ... indicates just how fully he committed his entire neurology and attention to the creative process. This same kind of 'hypnotic' quality ... has been observed in many other creative geniuses throughout history." (ibid)

As the Dreamer, Disney would relax his jaw, with his eyes staring fixedly at some point in space—usually up and to the right, a sign of visualizing. He also leaned forward on his elbows in a "feeling-oriented" posture, allowing his emotions to merge with his images. He leaned his cheek against the palm of his hand in the "telephone position" that often signifies internal conversation.

He could, apparently, simultaneously access visual, auditory, and kinesthetic representations in a synesthesia. He wrote that, while listening to music, he could see colors and images that represented the music, while feeling the movement and intensity. Disney felt a strong interplay of the senses.

Disney was excited by ideas. He was a visionary who relied on visual representations to foresee future possibilities for his art and his industry. In 1941, for instance, he wrote an article in which he predicted that cartoon shows would soon be commonplace on color televisions and that composers would create music specifically for animated features.

Disney maintained an optimistic viewpoint that he would achieve success, despite what he did not know and could not predict in his industry. He was always willing, therefore, to move ahead with plans and projects, hopes and dreams. A sense of excitement and discovery, the capacity for deep imaginative thought, combining the elements of sight, sound and movement, the desire for challenge and growth, an expectation of success, visualizing new possibilities—these are the traits of the Dreamer.

The Realist

Accessing the Realist state, Disney transformed ideas into reality. His mind held vivid characters, stories, and concepts. He brought them into a form that others could also experience and understand. He explored every project in depth, to make his images and stories realistic, believable, and meaningful to his audiences, thereby evoking identification and emotion.

He applied his artistic skills to make his creations match what he saw and heard in his mind. To perfect his skills, and those of his animators, he established an art school in his studio where he hired instructors in composition, anatomy, and locomotion.

Disney learned the technical aspects of his industry so that he could effectively apply the science behind the art. He welcomed technological advancements and innovations. He made sure that his productions not only kept pace, but forged new territory. His *Fantasia* was the first animated feature of its kind. Even today, decades later, it is regarded as a 1940s classic for its combination of art, music, and storytelling in motion.

Disney's strategy as a Realist was to turn each idea into a project and to manage each project with a plan. Then he monitored the progress of the project and the quality of the product.

He also perfected another skill: the ability to shift his perceptual position, in order to take on the mindset of each character in his stories. In NLP terminology, Disney could "associate" into his characters, taking on their personalities, views, and opinions. By doing so, he knew and experienced their motives, emotions, and behaviors intimately.

Disney formed a feedback loop between the Dreamer and the Realist. The Realist works with the mechanics of the creative process; acting on the original idea and checking in with the Dreamer as the work progresses. The Dreamer adds more details and figures out what was missing or unworkable in the original idea. While the Dreamer has a vision and a longer time horizon, the Realist works with a shorter time horizon and uses successive approximations to "chunk down" each element of the idea as it emerges into reality.

The Realist must patiently work through sticking points to complete each small facet of the project, often learning and refining while the work is in progress.

The Critic

Disney had an intense commitment to quality. He was known to carefully scrutinize every detail of a project as it neared completion, before giving final approval. His staff regarded his evaluations as formidable. He ordered revisions with an eye for perfection. He could spot the smallest inconsistency and insist on improvement and correction.

As the Critic, Disney often imagined himself as his audience. He associated into a child's perspective, as well as an adult's. He evaluated each product from his audience's point of reference, asking questions: Does it tell a good story? Are the characters convincing? Do the drawings and sounds portray each character with authenticity? Are there any "dead" spots in the story's flow? Are the event sequences logical? Is the product engaging and entertaining? Does it look right? Does it sound right? Would it hold a child's attention? Would it meet with adult approval?

At this evaluative stage of a project, Disney was known to seek others' views. He watched pilots of movies and cartoons with his entire production crew, opening the discussion to all opinions. He even consulted with maintenance workers and food service employees for "man on the street" opinions. Years later, in business circles, a similar practice became widely known as Total Quality Management.

The Critic evaluates and refines the Realist's product according to specific criteria, searching for mistakes, inconsistencies, problems, and possible consequences. The Critic also compares the Realist's product to the Dreamer's original concept, looking for what matches and what has deviated—assessing whether those deviations are improvements or flaws. The Critic is concerned with quality assurance, striving to correct any and every flaw before a product goes public.

Combining and Comparing the Three Approaches

You can determine from this discussion that the Disney Creativity Model requires a writer to possess the flexibility to shift comfortably between three approaches and to know which state is optimum at any given stage of a project. Dilts advised his readers to cycle through the three states in this sequence:

Dreamer: Visualize the concept.

Realist: Plan and organize. Apply skills and technology to transform the concept into a product.

Critic: Evaluate the product, determining what is needed or missing. Turn any problems over to the Dreamer as questions.

Dreamer: Respond to the questions by continuing to develop the concept. Turn additional ideas over to the Realist for implementation.

Realist: Apply skills and techniques to improve the product.

Critic: Evaluate the revised product and continue the cycle as needed.

I like to think of each state as a mindset. Inability to shift easily between these mindsets often bedevils inexperienced writers. The following table (adapted from Dilts, 1994) compares and contrasts the cognitive components of the Disney Creativity Model as they apply to writing:

Cognitive Components of the Disney Creativity Model

Cognitive Components	Dreamer	Realist	Critic
Attention	Vision	Action and Implementation	Logic
Cognitive Requirements	Imagination Creativity Curiosity	Knowledge Skill Technology	Quality Assurance Testing Refinement
Planning Approach	Options: Considers various approaches.	Procedures: Follows specific procedures to produce content.	Procedures and Options: Follows procedures to evaluate and revise content and considers options as they arise.
Perceptual Position	Self	Narrator Characters	Audience
Operational Modes	Thinks in terms of possibilities. Asks "What is possible?"	Thinks in terms of necessity. Asks "What is required?"	Thinks in terms of quality and improvement. Asks "How can this be better?"
Scope	Global: Broad concepts of the narrative.	Detail: Chunking down the task to produce the narrative.	Detail and Global: Zooming in on details, zooming out to evaluate global effects.
POWER Process Steps	Previewing (SPACE)	Organizing Writing	Evaluating Revising

The Creativity Cycle

Don't make the mistake of thinking of either the POWER Process or the Disney Creativity Model as linear. Both models are recursive, continually looping back to an earlier step or stage and then forward again as in the Creativity Cycle depicted in the following diagram.

The Creativity Cycle

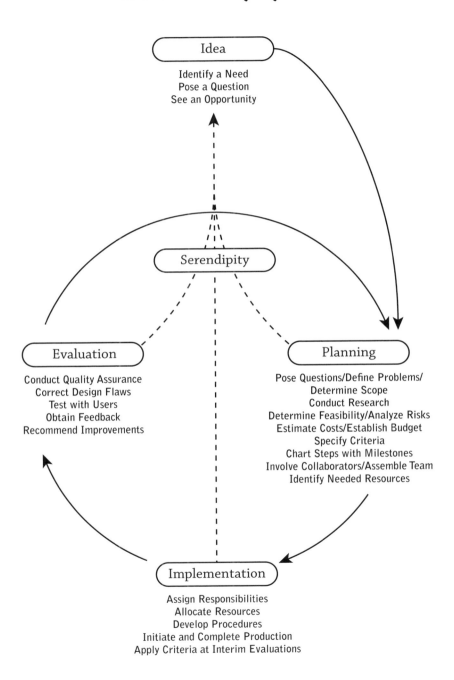

Idea
Identify a Need
Pose a Question
See an Opportunity

Serendipity

Evaluation
Conduct Quality Assurance
Correct Design Flaws
Test with Users
Obtain Feedback
Recommend Improvements

Planning
Pose Questions/Define Problems/
Determine Scope
Conduct Research
Determine Feasibility/Analyze Risks
Estimate Costs/Establish Budget
Specify Criteria
Chart Steps with Milestones
Involve Collaborators/Assemble Team
Identify Needed Resources

Implementation
Assign Responsibilities
Allocate Resources
Develop Procedures
Initiate and Complete Production
Apply Criteria at Interim Evaluations

As shown in the diagram, every creative endeavor begins with an idea, generated by a need, question, or opportunity. The next step is planning, followed by implementation and evaluation. The box under each activity shows examples of tasks that might occur in each phase of the project. You wouldn't require most of these tasks for an article or novel, but you might need them for writing a user's manual, a business plan, a research proposal, or a grant request.

In the Creativity Cycle, the writer (or team of writers) might cycle through the project several times, moving from planning to implementation, evaluation, and back to planning again for another development cycle. Notice that serendipity can occur at any of these three phases, when a new idea surfaces because of an unexpected need, question, or evaluative finding. The serendipitous idea that arises could eventually provide the impetus for yet another project and another creative cycle. In this way, companies develop "spin-off" products. The same thing happens in writing.

Every writer will have an idiosyncratic method for looping through the steps of developing an idea, planning the work, implementing the plan, evaluating the work in progress, and then repeating these steps, to the point of a finished product. Some will do it for every page, while others do it for each paragraph or each chapter. Eventually, you'll know what size chunk you feel most comfortable working with.

The worksheet for this chapter, in Appendix A, provides space for you to think about what each Disney state means to you and how you could apply each one to your writing. The next six chapters will describe how to access the Disney states while bringing the POWER Process to your writing. Along the way, you'll learn practical tips and strategies for improving your writing with NLP.

CHAPTER 4

For the Dreamer: Romance Your Idea

"It's an adrenaline surge rushing through your body. You have this spark of an idea that keeps threatening to burst into flames and you have to get the words out on paper to match this emotion or picture in your head."

Janet West

Everyone remembers the giddy, walking-on-air, near-delirium of falling in love.

That's how it is with Dreamers and ideas. Dreamers fall in love with ideas. They obsess, wonder, and fantasize about those ideas until they develop those ideas into a narrative. Dreamers get consumed with curiosity to find out where an idea will lead them. That curiosity drives research and interviews and historical investigation. The idea becomes something they need to share with others. Dreamers romance ideas.

In the Dreamer state, you become infatuated with an idea, as questions form in your mind. "What can I say about that idea? What else can I discover about it? Who else would want to know about it? How can others benefit from it? How can I develop this idea in an amazing way that holds people's attention?"

Romance is a trance—a focused state of rapt attention. Watch two people in love and you'll realize this. When you romance an idea, your mind develops a focus, picking up information related to that idea, like a magnet picking up iron filings. Your idea-based attention pushes and prods you to develop that idea into a book, an article, a report, or a web page. You'll notice relevant information and examples in unexpected places. Your mind will make connections and associations that surprise you.

What idea are you romancing right now? Your life experience will guide you to find the topics and ideas that intrigue you and shape your perspective. Let those ideas become your obsession. Let your mind get playful. See the potential in your idea. See it evolving into a product that others will enjoy. See it influencing others' actions and opinions. Let your creativity flow and move that idea from your head and heart onto the printed page.

Accessing the Dreamer State

A Dreamer envisions possibilities. Waking dreams are succulent morsels of imagination that whisper, "What if ... ?" There's a Dreamer in you. You can access your Dreamer now and whenever you want. Take the next few moments to relax and let your mind travel through the landscape of your memories as you follow this NLP strategy that anchors the Dreamer state:

1. Think back to a time when you watched something, or someone, feeling complete curiosity, wonder, and awe, tuning your senses to every nuance with fascination. Pretend you are there now, in the moment, seeing, hearing, and feeling. Take in every detail, so that you hold onto the feelings. Those feelings are elements of your Dreamer.

2. With those feelings of curiosity, wonder, and awe, step into another memory. This time, remember a moment of eagerness to learn something new. Remember having a "learner's mind": inquisitive and willing to explore. Be there now, reactivating those same feelings. Inquisitiveness is another element of your Dreamer. Let that inquisitiveness blend with curiosity, wonder, and awe. Hold onto those feelings and let them continue.

3. Now move your thoughts into a memory of playfulness—a moment of fun and laughter in which you could let your imagination run wild and silly. Be there now. See exactly what you saw. Hear exactly what you heard. Imagine doing it again and feeling the playfulness. That playfulness is an element of your Dreamer. Let that playfulness blend with curiosity, wonder, awe, and inquisitiveness.

4. Holding onto all those Dreamer feelings, return your thoughts to the here-and-now. Allow the deeper levels of your mind to recognize and memorize the common elements of those memories and feelings—feelings of curiosity, wonder, awe, inquisitiveness, and playfulness. Let all those feelings blend into the Dreamer state. Give yourself a cue for accessing this state: the word "Dreamer" will do just fine.

5. While continuing the Dreamer state, visualize an idea you've been entertaining—the topic you want to write about. Visualize it as a picture or symbol. Put it in the center of your visual field. Give it your full attention.

6. Breathe deeply and relax your muscles. Move the image of your idea upward into your visual field. Lean forward on your elbows, resting your right cheek in your right hand. Imagine the possibilities for this idea, how you could develop it. Visualize it unfolding. Let your imagination play with it.

Remaining in the Dreamer state, answer these questions:

> What possibilities does this idea hold?
> How do you want to develop this idea?
> What larger purposes can you accomplish with this idea?
> What readers will have an interest in this idea?
> What role could you take in sharing this idea with readers?
> What are some possible venues for sharing this idea with readers?
> What makes this idea worth writing about?
> What questions do you have about this idea?

Creativity Emerges from Living with an Idea

Dreamers think creatively. Neuroscientists attribute creativity to something called "intelligence memory" in which analysis and intuition work together to bring forth innovative outcomes (Duggan, 2010). Whatever we focus attention on attunes us to relevant information from a variety of sources. When new information comes in, the brain searches to see how it might fit with other information already stored in memory. When it finds a match, it combines remembered information with the new. While analyzing, the brain segments and stores information. When several pieces of information recombine into a new pattern, the result is a flash of insight—a burst of creativity!

Creativity begins with curiosity—the brain's state between knowing and not knowing. When the brain gets a new piece of information, it forms a new neural connection accompanied by a little rush of pleasure. The process of creativity engages out-of-consciousness mental resources (sometimes called "intuition"). The four steps are: 1) focusing on an idea or question, 2) reflection and searching for information, 3) illumination: the creative insight, and 4) motivation to act (Rock and Page, 2009).

In Chapter 1, I introduced L. Michael Hall, with his quote about writing prolifically. In an article titled "Games Prolific Writers Play" (Hall, 2001), he stated that many would-be writers rush off to write about an idea before they have "lived with" that idea. As a result, these hopefuls "write down half-baked ideas, ideas untested and untried in the crucible of other minds." Hall wrote:

> "What does it mean to live with an idea? It means to focus on it intently and really get to know it. It means to fall in love with that idea … to look at it from multiple perspectives, to turn it over and inside out, to explore the history of that idea, to delve into the hearts and minds of others who have danced with it … It also means to hang out with that idea when it is still formless, when it is vague, when your mind is a void about how to formulate it. It means living with ambiguity, confusion, and uncertainty for a while.
>
> Like a guy falling in love with a wonderful woman, and focusing intently on who she is, what she is like, her best qualities, it also means living with an idea when its flaws and imperfections come into view … The longer, deeper, and more intensely I live with a subject, the more ideas emerge, the richer the ideas become, and the more the insights come." (p. 23)

Living with an idea means exploring its dimensions and variations. One way to explore an idea is to read what others have written and said about it. Here are five additional ways to explore the dimensions of an idea:

- **Get up close and personal:** Get first-hand experience with your topic. If you want to write about Paris, go there. If you want to write a cookbook, get into the kitchen. If you want to write about golf, get your fingers around a golf club. Get acquainted with your ideas from the inside out.

- **Locate the experts:** If you aren't an expert yourself, locate people who are experts and talk to them. Interview them for their opinions, insights, and findings. Test out your conclusions with them. Get their advice.

- **Collect ideas in a box (or a file drawer):** I once interviewed a well-known speaker, author, and humorist, who told me how he developed ideas for his books and presentations. Whenever a topic sparks his interest, he assigns it to a cardboard box. When he reads a relevant article or section of a book, a copy goes into the box. When he hears a relevant conversation, joke, or story, he jots notes on a slip of paper—and into the box it goes. Greeting cards, news clippings, photos, anything that seems pertinent goes into the box. When the box is full, it's time to organize the contents and write. I do something similar, but I keep relevant information in file folders (hardcopy and digital).

- **Keep a writer's journal:** Journaling is a way to maintain your focus and keep track of ideas and insights while on the go. Maintain a paper journal or a digital one. List your contacts, citations, questions, and observations. Keep your journal handy because you never know when a new item of information will pop up.

- **Carry a recording device:** Some writers carry a portable voice recording device, such as a smart phone, to serve as an audio journal. Speaking extemporaneously into a recording device makes for spontaneity. You could even invite a friend to stimulate your thinking by asking questions and giving feedback while you are recording, so that you are sure to keep talking and adding content. If a question stumps you, it may point to a need for more investigation.

When you seize upon your idea, you'll notice, all around you, related information and events pertaining to your topic. Don't let those moments slip your memory, forgotten within days. Collect them in a box, a journal, an electronic recorder, a computer data file, or a filing system. Set aside shelf space in your home library for books on your topic and bookmark the pages you like. The ideas you collect will eventually flesh out your story and give it depth and vibrancy.

Develop Your Idea: The Mindmap and Storyboard

Once you've begun to understand your idea, it's time to develop it; to determine what you want to do with it, what you want to say about it. You might consider two ways to get the creative energies flowing: the mindmap or the storyboard.

The Mindmap: Mindmapping is a paper-and-pencil/pen method for organizing ideas around a central topic (Buzan, 1993; Wycoff, 1991). This method allows for non-linear thinking and encourages the free flow of ideas, unencumbered by the need for an outline.

Use mindmapping any time you feel stuck in organizing your ideas. You can mindmap an entire project and then make additional mindmaps for subsections or chapters, working at finer and finer levels of granularity. The key to a mindmap is to let your creativity flow without worrying about accuracy, order of content, or neatness. Here's how to do it:

1. Start with a large sheet of blank paper and a few colored pens. In the middle of your paper, draw a shape just large enough to contain a few words that describe your central concept. For illustration, let's say your central concept is Attracting Backyard Birds.

2. Surrounding the central shape, write key words that represent major topics related to your central concept. Examples could be: Backyard Habitats, Birdfeeders, Geography, and Seasonal Considerations. Draw lines branching out from the box or circle in the middle of the page, each pointing to a major topic.

3. Group relevant subtopics (using key words only) under each major topic. Let your brain dance and play with ideas as they come to mind. For example, under "Backyard Habitats" relevant subtopics might be: trees, shrubs, flowers, water, and sun exposure. At this point, your mindmap could resemble the illustration in the following diagram. Add subtopics and even tertiary topics until you've exhausted all ideas.

Attracting Backyard Birds

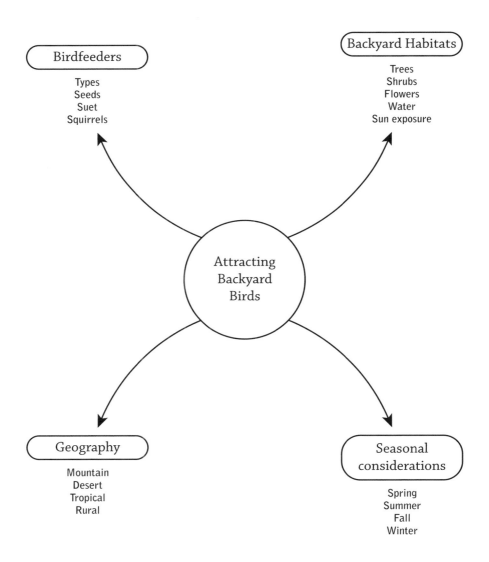

4. Draw arrows between related ideas. Use colors, symbols, underlines and highlights to create additional emphasis and associations among topics. When your mindmap is complete, it will resemble a wiring diagram. All your ideas will be displayed, categorized, and connected to one another on a single page.

5. Let your mindmap incubate for a day or two. Then evaluate it. Look at the balance among central topics and subtopics. If one topic seems weightier than the others, it could, perhaps, be divided into two or more subtopics. If one subtopic seems smaller than the others, perhaps that topic needs more information. Your mindmap might alert you to overlapping secondary or tertiary topics that could be combined. Finally, ask yourself, "Is anything missing?" to detect gaps in your selection of subtopics. Make changes as needed.

6. Decide on a logical sequence in which to present the major topics in your mindmap. Number these sequentially. These major topics will become chapter titles or major headings in your outline. The subtopics will form the content of each chapter or heading.

The Storyboard: Storyboards are especially useful for writing teams. Storyboards require a fairly large, flat, uncluttered space, such as a blank wall, cardboard flats, or a series of erasable white boards. Some teams cut large pieces of butcher paper and tape them up on the walls around the work space.

After a planning session, the storyboard is divided into portions; one for each major section of the project. The team divides into sub-teams, with each one taking responsibility for a section. The sub-teams are generally selected according to the specialties of the members. Each sub-team maps out their portion of the story, using words, sketches, photos, and sticky notes to convey the content. As the work progresses, sub-teams evaluate, compare, and critique one another's work until the entire storyboard achieves continuity, logical sequencing, and consistency.

Even as a solo writer, you could organize your content with a storyboard. You will see your entire writing project spread out before you, so that you can move portions, map out sequences, see relationships, and correct inconsistencies before you begin writing.

A mindmap or storyboard will provide direction for research and/or your outline, should you choose to make one. A mindmap is a handy tool to apply any time during the writing process when you feel stuck and unsure of how to proceed. You can mindmap an entire book and then each chapter with finer detail, even using a mindmap to brainstorm ideas for a single section or paragraph.

It's Preview Time

Now that you've fleshed out an idea, it's time to go to the Preview step of the POWER Process, to determine your SPACE: Self, Purpose, Audience, Code, and Experience. You'll find a worksheet (the Chapter 4 worksheet) in Appendix A. If you aren't sure how to describe any element of your SPACE, reread Chapter 2.

CHAPTER 5

For the Realist: Blast Past Writer's Block

"One of the main reasons for 'writer's block' ... is, I believe, that writers sometimes rush to the Realist stage of Dilts' model and try to start "doing" before they have envisioned their result. The second reason ... is the belief that what the writer writes should emerge perfect from their first typing. In Dilts' model, this means trying to run the Critic stage ... while doing the Realist job of writing."

Richard Bolstad

The American poet, William Stafford, once said, "There is no such thing as writer's block for writers whose standards are low enough."

You might think Stafford was berating successful writers for having low standards. Not so. *Unsuccessful* writers struggle with writer's block because they expect *too much* from a first draft. They freeze up, often in fear of making mistakes. They worry about seeming foolish. They torture themselves with scenarios about criticism, derision, and rejection. So they try to get it perfect from the get-go and end up feeling intimidated by a blank page. Knowing this, Stafford advised writers to lower their standards to get the creative juices flowing.

The message: the first draft doesn't have to be perfect. Just get something onto the page so that you can polish and refine it later on. To generate content, you must get into the Realist state. The Realist's job is to write. If you struggle with writer's block, you can breathe a sigh of relief. This chapter provides simple methods for conquering writer's block so that you can write with fluency. Lower your standards and let's begin!

Check Your Ecology at the Door: Reframing Writer's Block

Writer's block may be due to internal conflict. In NLP, we call such conflicts "ecological" issues. If you want to write, but you hold yourself back or get in your own way, it could be that you have an ecological conflict. To complicate matters, if you were taught to suppress negative feelings, such as anxiety or disagreement, your conflicts might reside out of your conscious awareness. They might prowl around in your unconscious mind, like dragons in their caves, just waiting to pounce on your efforts, spewing forth criticism and discouragement (Hall, 2000a).

Behind every ecological dilemma there is a positive intention. Your writer's block could be a protective mechanism based on normal, reasonable human needs and desires. Some positive intentions go toward preserving or obtaining something of value, such as feeling safe, secure, and accepted. Other positive intentions go in the direction of avoiding something risky, threatening, painful, or uncomfortable, such as criticism, embarrassment, failure, or rejection.

When you can express the source of your discomfort and figure out the positive intention behind it, then you can negotiate your way through the conflict. This method is better than beating yourself up for wrongly assumed inadequacies. The key to reaching resolution is to realize that you can write and still satisfy all those protective, positive intentions. In NLP, this negotiation process is called "reframing". It's a way to understand a problem, such as writer's block, in a new framework.

The steps below give you a way to understand the positive intentions of writer's block and satisfy them, while, nevertheless, eliminating all hesitation to write.

1. Sit quietly with yourself. Take time to tune in to your thoughts and emotions and answer these questions: When I feel blocked or stuck in my writing, what emotion am I feeling? What am I telling myself, that prevents me from writing? Acknowledge that dragon and allow it to speak openly.

2. Next, answer this question: What is the positive intention of my feelings? What am I worried about? What am I trying to avoid, protect, preserve, or prevent? Sometimes just acknowledging the source of a fear or anxiety (no matter how unrealistic or improbable it might seem) is sufficient to resolve the conflict.

    You could discover, or already know, that your discomfort about writing might be rooted in a past experience in which your initial attempts at writing, or self-expression, met with derision, criticism, or even punishment. If this is your situation, it helps to remind yourself, "That was then, and this is now. I survived that experience. Now I can release it. I can put it behind me because I'm older and wiser, with better skills and better ways to cope with such difficulties."

3. Appreciate that most shortcomings, writer's block among them, stem from an inner desire to perform well, receive positive regard from others, and preserve personal dignity. It may be reassuring to realize that you have such forces within yourself.

4. Ask yourself: How could I satisfy the positive intention in a more effective, alternative way? Answer this question and you can whack out that draft whenever you want to, giving full reign to spontaneity and creativity.

    It's best to answer this question intuitively, allowing the answers to surface from a deep inner knowing. A number of options and alternatives will, no doubt, surface. They will probably have nothing to do with writing competently, but, instead, with making sure that you feel comfortable in the *process*, at every Logical Level. This means your writer's block could be advising you to:

    - Establish a comfortable environment in which to write.

    - Make sure you've done adequate planning, preparation, organization and research.

    - Resolve other priorities that may be competing with writing.

    - Assemble the right tools and equipment for the job.

- Maintain a confident, playful, mindset untrammeled by irrational fears and limiting beliefs (more about those later in this chapter).

- Write first for yourself; writing for your readers will come later.

- Cultivate a relationship with at least one person who believes in you and your work and gives support, caring and encouragement. If you have such people in your life, turn to them often and reciprocate their affection and friendship.

- Stay connected to your purpose in such a way that it motivates you to write, despite the difficulties, setbacks, and hassles involved.

5. Make a commitment to absolutely follow through on the options and alternatives you seized upon in Step 4. Decide when and how you will do so. In a sense you are clearing all the mental obstacles you've put in your own way, so that you can let the words flow freely!

Later, in this chapter, we'll get to a strategy for accessing the Realist state. That's the state you need for generating content. But first, do you hear dragons growling?

Limiting Beliefs: Taming the Dragons of Fear

Writer's block is often based on fears generated by limiting beliefs that prowl the dark corners of the mind, blowing smoke that obscures coherent thought, and spewing forth negative self-talk that diminishes motivation and courage. The result: you procrastinate, you freeze up, your mind goes blank, and you wonder what delusions could have ever made you think you could write!

In Chapter 1, I described the importance of holding beliefs that instill confidence, persistence, and problem-solving. Another way to dismantle a limiting belief is to refute it with logic and replace it with an empowering belief.

In the sections that follow I've assembled the four most common fears that contribute to writer's block, each founded on a limiting belief. Each fear hides a positive intention to succeed, to perform well, to win respect, to feel satisfaction in a job well-done, and to avoid embarrassment or condemnation. You can tame these dragons. Soon those snorting, fire-breathing, overgrown reptiles will be purring like kittens and eating out of your hand!

Fear of Failure: This fear is often based on a belief that goes something like, "I'm bound to fail, so why try?" This dragon is particularly difficult to tame if you tend to think of *yourself* as a failure or if you feel discouraged by past events you regard as failures.

If you have ever thought of yourself, or anyone else, as a failure, consider this: failure cannot describe a person, because it is impossible to "fail" as a human being, since it is a given that human beings are inherently fallible to begin with. Failure can describe only the result of plans and actions. Failure says nothing about one's inherent worth or one's potential to succeed in the future.

Sometimes the Fear of Failure dragon might get in the way of planning and finding solutions to obstacles as they arise. This fear might lead you to decide that the outcome isn't worth the effort, time, and expense required. This fear suggests you should give up before you've even begun.

Here is a different way to think about failure. NLP defines failure as "getting a different outcome than the one you intended." The catch is that you'll never know what your outcome is until you produce it. Failure, then, functions as a source of information that can suggest areas for correction and improvement. Failure is not a signal to quit or give up. Failure presents an opportunity to do things differently to get another result.

In *The NLP Coach*, NLP coaching consultants Ian McDermott and Wendy Jago wrote that failure doesn't just happen. It is the result of interactions within a system of perceptions, beliefs, judgments, decisions, and actions. To understand the cause of failure is to examine the various elements in a situation as parts of a system that functions for good or ill. When you understand how your system or process is working for you or against you, then you have the means to structure things differently in the future (McDermott and Jago, 2001).

A relationship exists between actions and results. Success and failure leave a trail of clues as to what went right and what went wrong. Successful people have a distinct response to failure: they examine it with curiosity to retrieve useful information. They use that information to change their planning and decision-making. They define failure as an unexpected "detour" in the journey toward success.

Theodore Roosevelt wrote:

> "Far better it is to dare mighty things, to win glorious triumphs, even though checkered by failure, than to rank with those poor spirits who neither enjoy nor suffer much because they live in grey twilight that knows neither victory nor defeat."

You can tame the Fear of Failure dragon when you know that failure can never define who you are. You now have a strategy for coping with failure, should it occur, whatever form it takes.

Fear of Making Mistakes: Just like fear of failure, this fear comes out in negative self-talk that says things such as "I mustn't make mistakes," or "I have to get it right the first time," or "If I make mistakes, others will … (fill in your own consequence)." Fear of making mistakes is particularly difficult to contend with if you've been harshly criticized, unfairly chastised, or humiliated in the past for a mistake, with no recourse or way to defend yourself.

If you feel concerned with mistakes, you are not in the Realist state—you are in the Critic state. The solution is to access the Realist and be concerned solely with wrestling your creative ideas out of your head and pinning them down on the page, no matter how disheveled they may seem. The Realist state is for writing and producing content, so that later, as the Critic, you *will* find mistakes and correct them.

Following the POWER Process, you must produce a draft first, so that you have something to evaluate and revise. Writing a draft is often a process of experimentation, tinkering, guesswork, and trial and error. You must give yourself permission to make mistakes in the Writing step, secure in knowing that you'll correct those mistakes later in the Evaluating and Revising steps. After revising, turn your work over to a copyeditor or proofreader, who will, no doubt, point out additional mistakes and inconsistencies. A second pair of eyes is always valuable.

It is by our mistakes that we acquire some of our most enduring lessons. When you recognize mistakes and correct them (whether on your own, or with the help of a copyeditor, proofreader, writing coach, or teacher), your skills will rapidly improve. The more mistakes you make, the more you learn, and the better you get!

Fear of Criticism and/or Rejection: For writers, criticism and rejection do exist and take many forms. You get your tenth rejection from a publisher. A letter to the editor disagrees with your article. A colleague takes issue with your report. An editor, professor, reviewer, or supervisor is appalled by your latest offering. What makes your dragon roar?

The world would be a much nicer place if everyone adored and praised you and gobbled up your writing as though it's cherry pie! The unfortunate truth is that someone, sometime, somewhere will hand you a rejection, and will find fault with even your best effort. This dragon is a close cousin to Fear of Failure. This snarling lizard would have you believe that rejection and criticism are unbearable—a sure sign that you have no business in the world of talented people! You should turn in your keyboard and slump off into the sunset with your head hung down.

This dragon is a blowhard! It's time to grow a thicker skin that accommodates reality. Rejection and criticism are facts of life for every accomplished artist, performer and writer. They come with the territory. The only writers who don't get rejection and criticism are those who never submit their work. Do you intend to write and never show it to anyone? Only by risking rejection can you ever maximize your potential and accomplish success.

Rejection says nothing about your worth, potential, or talent. Rejection and criticism are sources of information that may suggest avenues for improvement, or another way to approach the problem. Many bestselling authors meet with numerous rejections until they learn what sells and how to pitch their ideas to editors, agents and publishers.

Rejections sometimes contain little useful information. "Your submittal doesn't fit with what we are looking for," doesn't really say how to improve. The proper response is to boldly shout, "Next!" Criticism, however, might give you specific insights that you can welcome and use to your advantage. In Chapter 9, you'll learn an NLP strategy of Responding Resourcefully to Criticism.

Fear of Inadequacy: This fear usually shows up in self-talk saying, in one way or another, that you aren't the right person for the task, you don't have the skills, talent, or credentials, or that whatever you produce will eventually be revealed as inadequate. This is the "not good enough" dilemma mentioned in Chapter 1.

Sometimes feeling inadequate comes from a faulty strategy of comparing yourself, unfavorably, to others who are more talented, intelligent, accomplished, or successful. It's a perfect formula for writer's block. Feeling inadequate by comparison, you can then berate yourself for your perceived inadequacies, assuming these inadequacies will continue into the future. Next, you can feel discouraged and depressed, freezing up, or procrastinating when it comes to writing.

The way to pacify this dragon is first to understand that while perfection is seldom obtainable, "good enough" is. Second, accept as a fact that there will always be others who are more talented, intelligent, accomplished, and successful than you are.

If you run this inadequacy strategy, stop, because it does not serve you. Everyone walks a separate life path in which talent, accomplishment, and potential are fluid and impossible to measure quantitatively. If you admire another writer's work, choose that person as a role model. Instead of comparing yourself to others, strive for personal best.

Resolve to continually learn, experiment, and take your skills to the next level.

By taming these dragons, you can blast through writer's block. Writer's block isn't due to a lack of talent; it's due to accessing the wrong state. Some people with writer's block get stuck in the Dreamer state, continuing to fantasize about an idea, but taking no action.

Others skip the Realist state and jump ahead to the Critic state. They start searching for flaws in the idea. They anticipate problems. They worry about what could go wrong. They criticize each new bit of content as it emerges, even before the draft has progressed to the editing stage. They stall out, striving for perfection instead of productivity.

Getting stuck in the Dreamer state or jumping ahead to the Critic state will not result in a finished draft. The next section will help you access the Realist state, so that you can start writing!

Accessing the Realist State

Think back to the last time you organized a complex undertaking, such as going on a long trip to a distant city. Perhaps, if you are a veteran traveler, you might think about many trips you've taken. What did you do in the planning phase? Did you consult others? Did you check maps or weather predictions? Did you evaluate travel options? Did you have a checklist so you could remember everything to pack? Did you let some people know when you would be away and tell others when you would arrive? How did you manage so many details?

And when you traveled, did you stay on schedule? Did you follow an itinerary? Did you find your way around? Or did you get lost and have to backtrack and try again? Did you have trouble figuring out unfamiliar accommodations, such as how to turn on faucets or lock the doors? Did you ask for help? At any point, did you revise your original plan? Did you keep track of things such as money, tickets, hotel room entry cards, passports, and luggage? Think back on the mindset you maintained for keeping track of things, adjusting to changes, applying your ingenuity, and figuring out solutions as you went along.

Managing details, working things out, and solving problems: these are the traits of the Realist. Dreamers romance ideas while Realists get the job done. The hallmarks of the Realist are focus, adaptability, and persistence. The Realist plans, organizes, juggles details, and manages the project. The Realist grapples with hundreds of tactical and artistic decisions that make for fluency and coherence. With persistence, the Realist stays on task, transforming a tangled mess of ideas into a well-crafted manuscript, ready for editing.

The Realist takes on the mindset of the technician or the craftsman. Like an architect who transforms a vision into a blueprint and then oversees the construction of a building, the Realist brings ideas to life. Here is a strategy for accessing the Realist mindset.

1. Recall a time when you turned an idea into a reality: when you developed a plan, executed the plan, step by step, and stayed on task until you achieved a result. Step into the memory and relive it. Remember where you were, what you saw, heard, and felt. Recall the concentration, the attention to detail, the eagerness to solve problems and answer questions, the way in which you applied your skills and motivated yourself to take action.

2. Return your thoughts to the here-and-now, but let the feelings and the frame of mind linger. You can anchor this feeling with a cue— the word "Realist" will do.

3. Now turn your thoughts to the idea or concept you envisioned in Chapter 3, when you accessed the Dreamer State.

4. Remaining in the Realist state, keep your head and eyes pointing straight ahead, while leaning forward slightly. Let a plan develop in your mind as to how you'll transform that idea into content. Visualize the components of the project and the specific actions you could take.

Having accessed the Realist state, how do you feel about taking action? Do you see yourself getting down to the task of writing? By the time you have completed this chapter, you should be ready to formulate your outline and begin writing content. In Appendix A, you'll find a

Chapter 5 worksheet for your outline, or you can simply make one up on your own. In the meantime, here are four tips to get beyond writer's block and start your Realist's creative juices flowing.

Four Tips to Get Beyond Writer's Block

Tip #1—Write Playfully

Write something! Write anything to get words on the page. Make it silly, make it wrong, but write! Write whatever comes to mind. Put on some upbeat music and dance around the room and sing out the words and then put them on the page.

Picture a little child jumping into a mud puddle with giddy abandon, getting dirty, and loving it! Write like that kid!

Tip #2—Brainstorm

You've heard of brainstorming. It's a good tool for teams. Teams brainstorm innovative solutions to problems. The leader poses a question: "How can we manufacture more widgets, without additional costs?" Team members call out any ideas that come to mind. All ideas and solutions are accepted without judgment. The leader, or a proctor, writes the ideas on a chalk board, or white board, or flip chart, for all to see. Members call out ideas until all possibilities are exhausted.

The group then eliminates the most problematic solutions, arriving at a narrow range of workable solutions. Members discuss the pros and cons of each solution, and how each might be improved. The team then reaches consensus on the best solution. They draw up an implementation plan, assign actions, and schedule another meeting for progress reports.

Brainstorming is great for teams because it allows diverse views and solutions to emerge. If you are a solo writer, you can brainstorm with yourself. Brainstorm anytime you feel stuck! Brainstorm a chapter, a paragraph, or even a single sentence! Pose a question and then just start generating possibilities.

Get away from the keyboard for a while. Stretch or take a walk in the fresh air, and just let your imagination run free with various solutions, options, and possibilities until you land on one that seems to work. Why not invite family and friends in on the brainstorming? Pose your problem to them and invite their responses. You might be surprised by answers you didn't expect!

Tip #3—Speed-write

Write for speed. Pretend you are in a contest to write as many words as possible in the next ten minutes. Don't stop to evaluate or revise. Just write as fast as you can think.

Tip #4—Jump Around in the Outline

You don't have to start at the beginning of your outline and move forward. Start in the middle and work outward, or start at the end and work backward. Jump around. Write a little here and a little there. Choose a section of your outline that most appeals to you at any given moment and write that section. As you fill in more sections, your draft will expand.

Move Away from Writer's Block

Writer's block is where frustrated, wannabe writers live. Every house on that block is home to untested and unexpressed ideas. Like agoraphobics, those ideas would love to see the light of day—to bravely sally forth into the world. Instead they languish because their authors haven't yet learned to access the Realist state. Those ideas can't get out and about because they are guarded by dragons!

You can tame those dragons and free your ideas for the world to see, hear, and read. When you begin writing, access your Realist and get down to work. The corrections, fact-finding, nit-picking, and resolving inconsistencies will come later. Let your first draft be something you write just for the heck of it.

Perfection isn't required.

Purr dragons, … purr …

CHAPTER 6

For the Realist: Get On Task and Stay There

> "Perhaps it would be better not to be a writer, but if you must, then write. If all feels hopeless, if that famous 'inspiration' will not come, write. If you are a genius, you'll make your own rules, but if not—and the odds are against it—go to your desk no matter what your mood, face the icy challenge of the paper—write."
>
> J. B. Priestley

If you want to continually feel motivated to write, identify what writing *means* to you—in terms of the process itself, the content you write about, the rewards you expect, and the contribution you hope to make. In my home library, there's a small book titled *101 Reasons Why You Must Write a Book* by Bob Burnham and Jeff McCallum (2006). Anytime I realize I'm avoiding a writing task or whining about how little money I make from writing (with apologies to my esteemed publisher!), I have only to flip through the pages of that book to be reminded of many reasons why writing matters to me.

As you identify the incentives that writing and publishing hold for you, you'll feel increasingly motivated to write, even when it means working through the difficult and inevitable sticking points. Here are a few reasons why people like to write:

- Getting published will improve your credibility, reputation, and expert status in your field of work.

- With the exposure you get from publication, you'll get additional referrals, customers, and sales for your business.

- You might get speaking engagements to talk about your subject matter.

- Your skill as a writer might advance your career.

- Writing is a means to self-expression and an outlet for creativity.

- Writing will improve your communication skills.

- Writing could bring opportunities to travel.

- Through writing, you can meet new people.

- Writing presents an ongoing challenge to learn and master the craft.

- Writing often generates income in advances, direct payments, and royalties.

- You will touch lives and inspire others with your unique message.

- You can write for altruistic reasons: to support a cause, raise awareness about something that matters to you, or to protest an injustice.

- Writing can lead to self-understanding and personal insight.

What is *your* overriding reason to write? Choose one that you can feel in the very fiber of your being. Make your reason match your highest values, cherished beliefs, goals, and purpose. Develop a message around ideas you can't wait to share. Let writing become your passion!

Once you have a driving reason to write, you need only apply motivational strategies that turn your ideas into action, propelling you from Dreamer to doer—a Realist. This chapter contains six NLP strategies that will ramp up your motivation, to keep you on task and intensely focused through every activity of the writing process. Read them over. Then choose one or two that you particularly like and apply them to your current writing project. Additionally, you can reflect on your own motivation to write with the Chapter 6 worksheet in Appendix A. I think you'll enjoy discovering for yourself how the right mindset can supercharge your ability to stay on task and get the job done.

Get Hooked on Writing with the New Behavior Generator

Would you like to get hooked on writing? The New Behavior Generator is ideal if you are unaccustomed to writing on demand or routinely to a set schedule. It is an NLP strategy for adapting a new behavior and feeling motivated to carry out that behavior consistently (Cameron-Bandler, Gordon, and Lebeau, 1985; O'Connor and Seymour, 1990; Hall and Belnap, 2004). Here is an adaptation of the New Behavior Generator for writing, in eight easy steps:

1. Answer these questions: What is your compelling reason for writing? What do you expect to get from it? What rewards or benefits are so appealing, so meaningful, that you are willing to put in the time and effort? State (or list) three highly-valued rewards or benefits that motivate you to write.

2. For each reward or benefit you identified in Step 1, imagine a scenario that demonstrates its fulfillment. Imagine exactly how it would be to realize the material rewards as well as the emotions. For each scenario, modify the visual and auditory details to make each one more and more desirable. For example, you could make the images three-dimensional and up close, with vivid details and bright colors. Make the sounds clearly audible with emotional overtones. Keep enhancing each scenario until you get a "wow!" feeling that brings a sweet smile to your face. Mentally move into each scenario so that you actually feel the enjoyment and satisfaction.

3. Identify *behaviors* that will lead to the benefits in Step 2: organizing, gathering information, writing, and anything else necessary to your project. Get specific about where, when, how often, and how long you will engage in these behaviors in order to have a finished product. Picture yourself fully immersed in these activities. Step into each image, so that you see, hear, and feel every component.

   As you imagine each behavior, picture the rewards and benefits scenarios that gave you a "wow!" feeling in Step 2. Fortify an association in your mind; each behavior in the writing process is the means to getting those juicy incentives! Keep switching your internal representations between behavior and reward, until imagining any writing behavior gives you a "wow!" feeling.

4. Access the Realist state, just as you did in Chapter 5. Think of a time when you have experienced this state of attention to detail, problem-solving, and persistence. The activity could be anything you do routinely: cooking meals, tending a garden, exercising, etc.

   Step into the memory of that behavior. Imagine you are there now, with all the sights and sounds, fully engaged in the action, aware of the essential thoughts that made it possible for you to put forth this effort consistently, time after time. As you relive that moment, be aware of your internal strategy for accessing this state. What do you think about? What do you tell yourself? What images do you hold in your mind? What beliefs support your behavior? How do you keep yourself on track? To what do you give attention and what do you ignore?

5. Bring your thoughts back to the here-and-now. Now transfer the Realist state to writing. Imagine a movie of yourself writing on your current project. Imagine you are the director of the movie. Watch the "you-in-the-movie" writing, checking notes, formulating ideas, and forging those ideas into words. Assume the you-in-the-movie has accessed the Realist state you experienced in Step 4, with the internal strategy to easily and consistently maintain that state.

   Make this movie just the way you want it. Make it attractive, motivating, inviting, and appealing.

6. Step into the movie, imagining you are there, in person. As the star of the movie, you are engaged in all the activities of writing, once more feeling that resourceful Realist state. See and hear the sights and sounds of your movie environment. What thoughts keep you on task? What beliefs do you apply? Bring in the scenarios showing the rewards and benefits of writing, as you intensify your desire to write.

7. Step out of the movie and return your thoughts to the here-and-now. Evaluate the quality of your state while you were in the movie (Step 6). Do you detect problems or areas to improve? What modifications would make writing even more essential, inviting, appealing, enjoyable, and compelling?

Play the movie through again with any improvements. Watch the movie, making sure each element meets with your satisfaction. Step into the movie again to test these improvements. See the sights and sounds, feel the emotions, have the thoughts, and feel the movement. Experience the concentration, the way you monitor your actions, or coach yourself, or keep yourself going. What do you say to yourself? How do you connect with those rewards and benefits you named and visualized in Steps 1 and 2? How do you feel afterward?

Repeat this step until your movie sizzles and you ABSOLUTELY MUST WRITE! You yearn to write! You feel eager to do it! You would even feel disappointed or upset if you couldn't do it. Exit the movie and return to the here-and-now.

8. Multiply the Realist state image into your future: imagine you are looking into your future, seeing the days ahead. Imagine that you have converted your mental movie (Step 7) to a DVD that you are now holding in your hand. Imagine that you've duplicated the DVD many times so that you have a huge stack of nearly identical DVDs—all movies of you writing, writing, writing away, with awesome motivation.

Pretend to cast that stack of DVDs out into your future so that the movie you have just visualized is now replicated again and again. The resourceful state you chose awaits you, growing stronger and more reliable as you move into each day. See instances in the future in which you are writing diligently, applying the Realist state, feeling motivated, enjoying it, and coming closer and closer to seizing those satisfying rewards and benefits!

Make Writing Irresistible with the NLP Godiva Chocolate Pattern

Richard Bandler developed the NLP visualization process called the Godiva Chocolate Pattern (Hall and Belnap, 2004). Its purpose is to make writing seem so irresistible, you absolutely must do it! The name comes from Godiva Chocolate, a confection so appealing some people cannot refuse it. In this pattern, you'll choose an activity that you *already* consistently find so pleasurable you feel compelled to do it. So choose something irresistible, as long as it is a *positive* in your life. With this NLP process, you'll soon apply the same "must do it" feeling to writing.

This pattern is structured around two images, which I'll designate as Image #1 and Image #2. Note that it also employs two visualization methods: association and dissociation. Association means that you visualize an experience in person; you are there. Dissociation means that you view the exchange as on observer, so that you remain somewhat emotionally neutral. Here are the steps:

1. Image #1: Visualize an activity you find so pleasurable you absolutely cannot resist doing it. Imagine moving into the image (association), so that the opportunity to engage in this activity is immediately available to you. Let yourself feel the desire, anticipated pleasure, passion, and absolute driving *need* to do this activity.

2. Clear your visual field, removing Image #1.

3. Image #2: Make a dissociated image of yourself writing. In other words, see yourself doing it (you are the observer, not the actor). Make the image contextualized and realistic looking.

4. Hold Image #2 (writing) in mind, while imagining Image #1 behind it. Image #2 hides Image #1, but you know it's there. Open up a tiny peep hole, in the center of Image #2, so that you can look through that hole to see Image #1, almost as though you are being pulled into it.

5. Visualize Image #2 (writing). Quickly open up the small hole in the center, so that you instantly see and move into Image #1. Get the full "must do it" feelings from Image #1.

6. Shrink the peep hole down quickly, so that you are looking again at Image #2 (writing), maintaining the feeling of desire and motivation engendered by Image #1. Let yourself have the feeling that Image #2 (writing) is irresistible, enjoyable, and so appealing that you have to do it.

7. Repeat Steps 5 and 6, three to five more times, as quickly as you can. Each time, visualize Image #2 (writing), peep through to image #1, get the feelings from Image #1, close the peep hole, and transfer the feelings to Image #2.

8. Clear your visual field. Visualize Image #2, without the peep hole, and notice how much more motivated you feel for Image #2 (writing).

9. Now prepare to have these same feelings in the future. Think about the next time you will write. Enter fully into the representation, and imagine you are there. Access the irresistible, "must do it" feelings.

10. Return your thoughts to the here-and-now. Anticipate future instances in which you eagerly sit down to write and enjoy it so much you can hardly pull yourself away!

Get into Action with the Mind-to-Muscle Pattern

The Mind-to-Muscle Pattern is a strategy that links well-reasoned understandings into a pattern that leads to action. It was developed by L. Michael Hall (Hall, 2000b) to bridge the gap between *wanting* to do something and actually *doing* it.

Identify any task that you *already* perform routinely and without fail. It might be going to work, or tucking your children in at night, or feeding your cat. You generally perform these actions routinely, without reminding, coaxing, or arguing yourself into it. You could say, then, that these habitual behaviors are the result of a mind-to-muscle connection. That's the kind of connection you can establish with this pattern.

In describing his rationale for the Mind-to-Muscle Pattern, Hall wrote:

"Ultimately, personal mastery arises from the ability to turn highly ... valued principles into neurological patterns. As with typing ... the original learning may take a considerable amount of time and trouble in order to get the muscle patterns and coordination deeply imprinted into one's muscles. Yet once we have practiced and trained ... then the learnings become incorporated into the very fabric of the muscles themselves ... At that point we have translated principle into muscle." (p. 238)

The Mind-to-Muscle Pattern converts procedural patterns into physical experience in which you *feel* the need to *act* on an objective you regard as worthwhile. In this chain-like process, you move from understanding, to belief, to decision, to emotion, and to action. Here are the steps:

1. **Principle:** Identify a principle associated with writing. What makes writing meaningful and worthwhile to you? What makes you *want* to do it? Choose a principle that is true and reliable. State your principle in a way that is succinct and compelling. Here's how— make your principle into a sentence that begins: "I write because I understand ..." What do you understand about the *value* and *purpose* of writing that makes it worth doing? Example: "... writing is a way to share my passion and help people ... (whatever you help them to do)."

2. **Belief:** Describe the principle as a belief. What do you absolutely *have* to believe in order to feel *driven* to write? State the belief with a sentence that begins: "I firmly *believe* ..." State this belief convincingly. Example: "... people need my message and I am the best person to express it to them."

3. **Decision:** Would you like your actions to reflect that belief? What decision would result? Reformat your belief as a decision, expressed as a sentence that begins: "From now on, I choose to ..." State exactly what you intend to do. Example: "From now on, I choose to write and revise daily on my project and finish it." Say this sentence convincingly and congruently to yourself.

4. **Emotion:** If you are completely congruent in your decision, what emotion would you inevitably feel? Let yourself have that feeling right now. Notice the emotion, your posture, your breathing, and other physical responses. Rephrase your decision as a mind-body state. Construct the sentence this way: "With my decision to ... I

feel … and I experience …" Example: "With my decision to write and revise daily, I feel eager to make progress, I feel pulled to do it, and I experience an urgency to express my ideas and my message."

5. **Action:** What action will naturally follow from the principle you understand, the belief you hold, the decision you've made and the emotion you feel? State a specific action you will take today as an expression of the above steps. Start your statement this way: "Today, as an expression of my principles, my belief, my decision, and my feelings, I will …" Finish that sentence by saying, with conviction, what you will do—your next action toward finishing your current project.

6. **Visualize:** Visualize the action you *will* take today. Imagine that you move into the image; doing, seeing, hearing, and *feeling compelled* to do it. Make your image irresistible, so that you feel you must do it. Visualize taking action every day until your project is finished to your satisfaction.

7. **Consolidate:** Consolidate the elements of this pattern by repeating the principle, the belief, the decision, and the emotion while continuing to visualize your action. "Today I will … because I understand that … and I believe … and I've decided … and I feel …" And what will you do the day after that? And what other actions will you take? What do you understand? What do you believe? What have you decided? How do you feel? When will you do it? How often will you do it?

The Mind-to-Muscle Pattern forms an emotional attachment to a resulting behavior, by associating it with a valued principle, a belief, a decision, and a feeling. With such a combination, you can't help but take action, don't you agree?

Walk Your Future Time Line to Develop Positive Expectations

Imagine one of your goals as writer. Imagine it is a magnet, pulling you forward, toward its fulfillment.

When people maintain images of their goals, assigning a specific point in time for the accomplishment, they become more goal-oriented. They feel intensely motivated to put forth effort toward their goals. They approach each step in the process with the end result in mind.

Time-Lining (Hall and Bodenhamer, 1997), also known as Time Line Therapy (Andreas and Andreas, 1991; James and Woodsmall, 1988), is an NLP process for, among other things, accessing resourceful states while envisioning one's goals. Time lines are idiosyncratic, three-dimensional representations of the flow of time and personal events in the past, present, and future.

What do you want to accomplish as a writer? Make a picture of your goal accomplished. You might see yourself speaking at a professional conference, or at your book-signing, or smiling while holding up a magazine containing your article, or seeing your screenplay in production.

One way to get focused and stay focused on a goal is to see it on your future time line. In this way, you "program" your expectations and actions to align with your goal, increasing your motivation and persistence. Here's how to do it.

1. Visualize your time line—imagine seeing your future time line stretching out ahead of you, as a linear image. You might see your future time line as a path or a beam of light. Designate a location and date on your future time line where you place the image of your goal, fully accomplished.

2. Imagine that you step forward on your time line, walking into your future, toward your goal. With each step you take, imagine the behaviors you'll engage in to produce your goal. Let each step represent a milestone in the process. Visualize each one. As you get closer to your goal, let your desire to achieve it get stronger.

   Let images form around you as you visualize the activities of writing—collecting data, formulating an outline, crafting your product word by word and page by page, editing, polishing, and then moving through the publishing process. Continue moving forward on your time line until you see before you the result—a published work.

Step into the moment when your goal is achieved. Feel the exhilaration! Imagine how you are celebrating your success and sharing your joy with others!

3. Look backward from this imagined vantage point in the future, back to the present, when you first visualized your goal. Imagine that you see markers on the time line leading from then (the present you left behind) to now (your position in the future) that represent the milestones you completed in reaching your goal.

   Visualize pictures of yourself at each milestone, completing the phases of the project. See that you applied discipline and skill. You persisted in spite of delays, interruptions, and obstacles. You solved problems as they arose. You accessed the Dreamer, the Realist, and the Critic with flexibility and ease. Let your imagination reverse-engineer the effort and creativity you demonstrated to accomplish your goal.

4. Return to the present. As you did in Step 1, see your future time line stretching out ahead. See your accomplished goal in its designated location, waiting for you. Notice what has changed. Now that you know what actions to take, and where those actions will lead, your imagery might be different. Perhaps you have now programmed your mind with expectations that will cause you to notice something useful that you didn't notice before, while you feel the imperative to write more and more each day.

Flow: Write with Your Brain in Alpha Frequency

In 2011, I interviewed Roy Hunter, an internationally renowned hypnotherapist, trainer, and author, for an article I was writing (Pearson, 2011). I interviewed him about his experience in training hypnotherapy practitioners and how he developed his curriculum and taught it in a community college. At the end of the interview, I complimented Roy on his many published books, asking about the secret behind his prolific writing.

He said that he writes "with both sides of the brain." I asked him to explain. He said when he writes a book, he starts with an outline and a general idea of the content for each chapter. He writes one chapter at a time. As he sits down to write a chapter, he puts himself into a hypnotic trance (which he attributes to the right side of the brain) to write the rough draft. Then he comes out of trance to edit what he has written (attributing this activity to the left side of the brain).

I asked him how he gets himself into a hypnotic trance. He said he first sets up a "peaceful place trigger." Here's how he described it:

> "Close your eyes and imagine a beautiful place of sights and sounds and feelings that are calm and peaceful. You touch your thumb to your finger that you establish as your 'peaceful place' finger. Then you take a deep breath and you think the word, 'Relax.'"

Then he described how to write while in a peaceful state.

> "So when I get ready to write, I take myself to a peaceful place, think the word 'relax', touch my thumb to my finger, and then I focus on my intention for that chapter, section, or article, depending on what I'm writing. Then I let my fingers do the typing ... I'm guiding the movement and letting the process flow. I'm focusing on what I want by inducing a light trance and excluding distractions. I need at least 15 minutes of uninterrupted time to do this, so as not to break the trance."

Hunter has perfected the art of writing while in trance. Neuroscientists know that trance occurs when the brain is operating in the alpha frequency: a brain state in which electromagnetic activity slows, allowing enhanced imagination, concentration, and absorption, while quieting the emotions. Trance states occur naturally and spontaneously whenever we daydream, or fantasize, or get "lost in thought," or caught up in a good movie, an exciting novel, a fascinating conversation, or exquisite music.

For many established authors, writing is a state of focused reverie, where their concentration is so intense it seems the words, the page, and the narrative are all that exist in the moment. All else seems to recede into the background. Even time's passage is ignored.

This special state of intense absorption and intrinsic motivation is the "flow" state, so named by psychologist Mihaly Csikszentmihalyi. The flow state depends on a balance between the demands of the task and the skills of the performer. A task that is too difficult prompts discouragement. A task that is too simple prompts apathy. When a task seems challenging, but doable, it becomes engaging. The flow state accompanies peak performance in any endeavor. That's why it's a good idea to hone your skills on moderately challenging assignments prior to taking on your masterpiece.

Perhaps you are now wondering how it would be to write while in the alpha frequency of flow.

Meet Your Future Self—A Published Author!

Of all the forces that shape sustained action and persistence, identity may be one of the strongest. It is your sense of self, governing what you do, say, and think when feeling most congruent and authentic. Identity flows and changes throughout our lives: who we've been, who we are, and who we are becoming.

Identity creates emotional attachments to specific activities that can captivate your attention and energies. When you believe you are a writer, or are becoming a writer, you are inclined to think, speak, act, and have emotions in specific ways that seem consistent with that belief. You do what it takes to do what writers do. You tackle your ideas and wrestle them onto the page until they say "uncle"—or whatever you want them to say.

Mentally construct an image of yourself in the future, when you have proof that you are a writer. See this "future you" holding up a finished product, happy with the attendant rewards. You might see this future you with a publishing contract, or speaking about your work at a professional conference, or greeting guests at your book signing. You might see this future you pointing to an article with your byline, or presenting your proposal to your company's customer.

Notice that this future self has accomplished what you have set out to do. Mentally move forward in time and step into the shoes of this future you. Imagine how it feels to have already put forth the necessary effort to reach this moment (in the future). Imagine how it feels to have this accomplishment. Think about the steps you took to complete your project—the planning, the writing, and the revising.

Remember how you applied persistence and tenacity, coaxing yourself through the rough spots, coping with the difficulties. Think about how much you have learned. These thoughts and feelings can remain with you, even when you return, mentally, to the present, planting seeds of motivation.

As you bring your thoughts back to the present, reconstruct the image of that future you. Imagine a conversation with this future you, who seems quite willing to guide and advise you. Imagine the questions you might ask:

> What is my next action on this project?
> How can I improve on my plan?
> What have you (future self) learned that I have yet to know?
> How can I move through discouragement?
> What is the main problem I need to solve and how shall I do it?

Allow the answers to enter your mind intuitively, as you imagine your future self "responding" to each question, telling you how to proceed. You can turn to this future you for guidance and encouragement. He or she is just a few steps ahead of you, in time, forging the path and showing the way: a friend, mentor, and coach.

CHAPTER 7

For the Realist: Write for Your Reader

"My task ... is, by the power of the written word to make you hear, to make you feel—it is, before all, to make you see. That—and no more—and it is everything."

Joseph Conrad

You've been writing your heart out for a few pages or a few paragraphs. You feel pretty good about what you've written. Maybe you like the way you've expressed concepts and ideas, the way you've moved the narrative along. At times you might even have felt astute or clever with the way you've turned a phase or made an analogy.

Nevertheless, at the back of your mind, there is one nagging question. What will my readers think of it? How will they respond?

That's what this chapter is about—successfully getting your ideas into the heads of your readers, making them believe you, agree with you, like your stuff, see the benefit, and buy what you are selling.

Who is your intended reader?

You will recall that in the POWER Process, one of the steps in Previewing is to define your audience. Who is your reader? What kind of person are they? What does this person want, need, and expect from you?

Your reader is the ultimate judge of the value of your content. Writing with your reader in mind, you might be wondering:

How can I make her understand?
How can I "package" my ideas to appeal to him?
How can I make her believe me?
How can I win his heart and mind?

How? Make it real. Make it relevant. Make it readable. Make it understandable.

Recall the NLP principle: the meaning of your communication is the response you get. It means that as a communicator, *you* are responsible for your reader's response. If you communicate in a way that your target readers don't "get it," then you haven't yet communicated in way that evokes the response you want.

"But wait," you say. "How can I predict how others are going to respond?" Good question. I wish I'd thought of it myself.

Here's the solution: know your readers and write in their 'language." In NLP, we call this rapport-building. Rapport creates an interpersonal connection. It is the foundation of trust, credibility, and influence. Rapport stimulates feelings of kinship and bonding. Through words, writers create rapport with their readers.

Every beginning student of NLP learns about rapport. It is the essential first step in effective communication. It requires that your message matches your reader's world view and communication style. Rapport creates a harmonious relationship between you and the reader.

Writers know something about their readers, because they generally write for people like themselves. They write for readers in their own profession or for readers with whom they share opinions and interests. They ask the questions their readers would ask.

If you don't know your typical readers, it behooves you to do so. Mingle with them. Join their social and professional circles. Interview them. Read what they read. Learn to speak their language—meaning that you communicate in ways that are relevant and sensible to them.

Rapport matters; especially when you want to convince people to do something—buy a product or service, agree with a policy, support a cause, learn a process, or vote for a candidate. Most people think of rapport as happening in face-to-face conversation, or in voice-to-voice conversation.

In NLP training programs, trainees learn to get into rapport by observing another's breathing, posture, facial expressions, gestures, and eye movements, and listening for voice variations (pitch, tone, pace, and volume). By mirroring physical cues and matching voice variations, trainees learn the beginnings of rapport. By listening to others and summarizing their content, trainees learn the basics of empathy.

As a writer, you can't see or hear your reader, except in your imagination. Your challenge is to build rapport (and possibly express empathy) through word-to-eye conversation. This chapter will teach you how.

Describe Your Target Reader

Describe your target reader for your current project. How does your reader see herself? What makes him tick? What makes her feel unique? What are her likes and dislikes? What are his problems and concerns? What do you know about your reader's qualities and strengths?

What does your reader want from you? Why would your reader care about what you have to say? What do you want your reader to think, do, and feel? How can you get him to have that response? You can answer questions about your typical reader with the Chapter 7 worksheet in Appendix A.

You might be aware that to answer these questions, you have to put yourself in your reader's shoes and see the world through his eyes, think like she thinks, and feel what he feels. For that, you'll need to shift your perceptual position.

Take Your Reader's Perspective with the NLP Perceptual Shift

Most writers, I believe, write for themselves first and then for their readers. Which is as it should be, to my thinking. Writing from your own point of view, in NLP parlance, is writing from "first position." This is how to get words onto the page.

Making your content palatable to your reader requires that you shift to your reader's perspective. In NLP, it's called a "perceptual shift" to "second position"—taking the point of view of the person with whom you are communicating. Here are the steps:

Step 1—Visualize your typical reader

Imagine your typical reader sitting across from you. You might be thinking of someone you actually know, or a composite reader you've never met. Picture the face, hair, shoulders, arms, and hands. Visualize that the two of you are looking at each other, making eye contact. You both have the same breathing and posture and facial expression. The two of you are in rapport.

Step 2—Take your reader's position

Now shift into your reader's position. Imagine that you put yourself into the mind of your reader. Pretend you can think her thoughts and feel her emotions. Pretending that you are now the reader, read over what you've written. Here are some questions you might ask yourself, from the reader's perspective:

- As the reader, what are you hoping for?
- How does the writing evoke your thoughts and feelings?
- Do you understand the concepts?
- Do you know what the writer wants you to do?
- Do you understand the writer's purpose?
- Do you understand where the writer is going?
- Do you feel, within yourself, any resistance, confusion, or disagreement?
- Has the content offended your sensibilities in any way?
- Have you encountered any jargon or scientific/technical words that you don't understand?
- Do you understand the references to people, places, events, and axioms?

Step 3—Return to your own position

Return to your perceptual position as the writer, bringing along whatever you learned in Step 2. Let your reader's perspective guide your revisions.

Skillful writers frequently shift between their own and their reader's position, automatically, unconsciously, and effortlessly, to continually check on their writing, with the reader in mind. They develop the ability to write as though the reader is right there, reading along, looking over their shoulder. As you write and revise, frequently check in with your imagined reader.

Rapport implies that you select metaphors, analogies, examples, aphorisms, humor, and references to people, places, and events that your reader can understand. If you introduce a new or unfamiliar idea, word, process, or concept, explain it. If you want to teach your readers something, first relate it to something they already know. Help your readers apply your information to their circumstances.

You can also create rapport with your readers and get them engaged with your content by stimulating their senses and matching their internal representations: visual, auditory, kinesthetic, and olfactory/gustatory. But first, you have to get their attention.

Openings: Grab Their Attention

Successful writers manage somehow to get into their reader's heads. When it comes to relating to your reader, there's another skill at which you should excel. It's the ability to seize your reader's attention.

People are overloaded with information. Every day, your targeted readers are inundated with hundreds of bits of information, all vying for attention. Why should they stop to read yours? What will make your piece stand out from the competition? What will make your piece something your reader *wants* to read?

The answer is to grab the reader by the lapels and say, "Look here, read this!" You can do it with titles, headings, and opening sentences. The stipulation is that your "attention-grabber" should relate to the subject matter and prepare the reader for what's to follow. Here are 20 ideas for getting your readers to sit up and take notice:

1. Describe the reader's current situation or circumstances

2. A thought-provoking question

3. An emotion, expressed as a single word, followed by an explanation of who felt that emotion and why

4. A recent headline from the news

5. A tie-in to a current season or holiday

6. An invitation to guess something

7. A short questionnaire or quiz to test the reader's knowledge

8. A promise to share a secret or reveal a mystery

9. An amusing play on words

10. A reference to, or an excerpt from, a well-known story, fable, play, movie, song, poem, myth, or historic event

11. A twist on a familiar proverb, cliché, or axiom

12. Disagree with something everyone knows to be true and then explain

13. A description that paints a picture in the mind's eye

14. A quote from a well-known person

15. A story

16. Ask the reader to remember or imagine something

17. A clever analogy

18. A short, declarative statement

19. A warning to readers concerning what they are about to read

20. A little-known but startling fact or statistic

Choose Words that Match Sensory Modalities

Consider this paragraph:

> "The quiet, cool darkness of the bar was a welcome relief from the scorching afternoon heat and the noisy, crowded street. I gave out a

long sign of relief as I slid onto the barstool and propped my elbows onto the countertop. I could feel the wet shirt clinging to my back as I leaned forward and rubbed my forehead with my fingers. As my eyes adjusted to the dim light I could hear the murmurs of private conversations, occasionally punctuated by a burst of laughter or profanity. The air was thick with the smells of spicy food, beer, cologne, sweat, and cigarettes. I could hardly wait to get my hand around a cold beer and pour it down my throat."

Did you make a picture in your mind? Descriptive writing uses sensory-based words (among other techniques) to evoke the reader's imagination and emotions (Marius, 1998). Such words create movies in the reader's mind. Successful fiction writers and storytellers excel at this. They tell the reader what the protagonist sees, hears, smells, and tastes; his or her physical sensations, thoughts, movements, and emotions. Such vicarious experience prompts the reader to automatically identify with, and care about, the central character.

Knowing what you now know about internal representations, you understand that people mentally recreate their experiences in the external world through four primary sensory modalities: visual, auditory, kinesthetic, and olfactory/gustatory.

People also process information through these modalities, revealing that process in sensory-specific words called "predicates." Thus, one person will say, "I *see* your point," while another will say, "I *hear* what you're saying," A third will say, "I *grasp* your meaning." A fourth might say, "You've given me a *taste* of what I came here to learn." Predicates can communicate literally or figuratively.

It seems that many people possess a preference for one modality over another, especially when it comes to learning and remembering. You've probably read or heard that visual learners seem to do best when they can observe. Auditory learners are good listeners. Kinesthetic learners benefit from hands-on learning and participation.

One could speculate that visual readers enjoy vivid descriptions that paint word-pictures in their minds. Auditory readers attune to the way words and word combinations sound. Kinesthetic readers warm to action words.

It may be closer to the truth to say that most people can learn and process information through whatever modality they encounter, and probably learn exquisitely through a *combination* of modalities. Considering the diversity of information processing preferences that will no doubt exist among your readers, it's a good idea to use a variety of predicates in your writing. The following table gives a few examples of predicates in each modality.

VISUAL	AUDITORY	KINESTHETIC	OLFACTORY GUSTATORY
Visualize/Watch	Talk/Listen	Feel/Sense	Taste/Smell
An eyeful	After-thought	All washed up	Smells fishy
Appears to …	Blabber mouth	Boils down to	Smell a rat
Cast a shadow	Rings a bell	Come to grips with	Leaves a bad taste
Bird's eye view	Clearly expressed	Wrestle with	Sweet/Sour
A dim view	Call on	Cool/Calm/	Tartly
Eye to eye	Earful	Collected	Bittersweet
Flashed on	Give an account of	Firm foundation	Repugnant
Get a perspective	Grant audience	Floating on air	A whiff of …
Get the full scope	Heard voices	Get a handle on	Fragrant
Hazy idea	Whispers a	Get the drift	Aromatic
Colorful personality	message	Hand in hand	Minty-fresh
In light of	Hold your tongue	Hang in there	Gobble
Look/See	Idle chatter	Cold/Hot	Lip-smacking
Make a scene	Loud and clear	Hold	A snootful
Mental image	Manner of	Rough/Smooth	Nosey
Paint a picture	speaking	Irritating	Morsel
Naked eye	Speaks to me	Keep your shirt on	Chew the fat
Observe	Resonates	Lay cards on table	Cut your teeth on
See to it	Out-spoken	Light-headed	Sink your teeth into
Short-sighted	Purrs like a kitten	Moment of panic	Nibble
Showing off	Rap session	Walk the path	Delicious
Sight for sore eyes	Tattle tale	Pull some strings	Scrumptious
Staring into space	Tongue-tied	Slipped my mind	Mouth-watering
Tunnel vision	Tune in/tune out	Sharp as a tack	Bitter pill to
Face to face	Unheard of	Stiff upper lip	swallow
Shadowy	Voiced an opinion	Topsy-turvy	Salivating
Look it over	Within hearing	Comfort	Bland
	range	Bounce/Jump	Succulent
	Give a listen to		
	Musical/Melodic		

Suppose your subject matter appeals mostly to one sensory domain. An article on food and cooking, for example, might appeal mainly to taste and smell. In this case, you could first select predicates that match the sensory domain. You could write about the tangy taste of cinnamon, for example. Then slide over into other predicates, adjectives, and adverbs so that your subject matter engages all the senses. Wine connoisseurs do this when they talk not only about the tastes they find in wines, but the fragrances, texture on the tongue, color, clarity, and viscosity. They even compare wines to a melody with the "notes" of various flavors.

Now do this. Think about whatever project you are working on at the moment. Visualize your reader absorbing the information, eyes scanning the page, lingering on the words; focusing on their meanings. Hear the reader whispering occasional remarks to the self, whenever a specific passage speaks clearly and sends echoes through the chambers of their imagination. Take your reader's place and feel your pulse quicken with excitement as the mind dances with the message and its implications. Do you sense the subtle change in breathing as you grasp a new idea? Perhaps now you understand, first hand, how sensory modalities intensify the ways in which your reader consumes your information.

Lead Readers Where You Want Them to Go

In NLP, rapport is the first step in understanding and bonding with your audience. The next step is to pace and lead. To pace with readers is to convey that you understand them or that you are like them. Communicate that you know what they like and dislike, their strengths and weaknesses, their triumphs and disappointments, their background and characteristics, their concerns, needs, and wants. To lead is to then steer them in the direction of your message, thesis, recommendation, or solution. One way of thinking about pacing and leading is: meet them where they are and take them where you want them to go.

Pacing and leading goes beyond rapport and empathy. To pace and lead is to align your intent with your reader's situation, needs, and expectations.

There is a familiar adage in the world of marketing: "Every customer is tuned in to one radio frequency: WIIFM (What's In It For Me?)." Whether you are marketing or not, your readers are your customers. If you want to convince them of something, make your message match their beliefs and values, hopes and aspirations. Commiserate with their problems and challenges. Then show them how it is to their advantage to take your recommendation or to implement your solution. Provide proof. If you want your readers to take action, spell out clearly what you want them to do. In marketing, this tactic is the "call to action."

Make your message meaningful, useful, and relevant. Use phrases that make it clear how your ideas connect to the reader's needs and concerns. Examples are:

- The best way to accomplish this is …
- … so that you can …
- This is important because …
- Here's what this means to you …
- Here's the solution …
- The benefit to you is …
- The point of telling you this is …
- There's a moral in this story.
- What you should remember is …

Put yourself in your reader's position and ask, "Why should I care?" Then make them care.

Tell a Story

Anthropologist Gregory Bateson had a strong influence on the early development of NLP, pointing out hierarchical elements of learning, change, and communication. He contributed theoretical understandings about behavioral modeling in general and the NLP Logical Levels in particular. An anecdote is attributed to him that has undergone numerous variations over the decades. Maybe you've heard it. The punch line is always the same. The story goes like this …

Some scientists got together to build the world's smartest computer. They worked doggedly for many months, applying all their skills and knowledge to the arduous task. When they finished the effort, they stood back to admire their work. Then one of them asked the computer a question: "Do you compute that you will ever be able to think like a human being?" After much processing, the computer displayed a response: "That reminds me of a story ..."

Bateson observed that one of the distinguishing characteristics of human beings is that we are storytellers. We learn and share our culture through stories. The oldest cave drawings tell stories. Stories surely existed before the written word as a way of preserving and transmitting knowledge.

Everyone loves a good story. Stories entertain, teach, evoke emotions, inspire, and bestow vicarious experience. Stories can help us understand cause–effect and how to solve problems. Stories make the message memorable because they captivate the imagination. Tell stories not for the sake of telling them but to amplify the message—to underscore the point.

The developers of NLP noted the communication value of stories when they observed the way the legendary psychiatrist, Milton H. Erickson, performed hypnosis. In his later years, Erickson seldom conducted formal trance inductions. He merely sat hunched over in his wheelchair, looking intently at his listener, droning on in his gravelly voice. He seemed to ramble from one story to the next, talking about everyday matters that reflected some aspect of the listener's situation. The listener eventually went into a hypnotic state, to emerge and find within days that the problem had resolved itself or had disappeared altogether. Erickson became known as a master of therapeutic storytelling. You'll read more about him in Chapter 10.

Stories are everywhere. They are in the daily news, embedded in world events, and in the unique happenings of your own life. Some family stories are handed down from one generation to the next. Walk through any city or any neighborhood and you'll find stories for the telling. People make sense of their lives by telling their stories. Listen for stories whenever people get together for friendly conversation. Depending on your purpose and your audience, you can create variations on well-known stories from history, fairy tales, folk lore, mythology, scripture, and classic literature. Here are some recommendations for crafting a memorable, meaningful story:

- **Decide your message first.** Then choose a story that gets your message across to the reader. Your story should illustrate the point of your message.

- **Determine the effect you want to have on readers.** Will your story entertain, persuade, amuse, inform, inspire, or challenge readers?

- **Construct your story with a clear starting point, body, and ending.** Start with an opening that sets the time and place, tells the reader what to expect, and/or captures their attention, imagination, or curiosity. Make the content of your story relevant to your readers' concerns, expectations, and level of comprehension. Don't let your story trail off at the end. Choose a strong closing that lends finality with a summation, a message, or a punch line.

- **Create mental images in your reader's mind.** Activate imagination with vivid descriptions that evoke sensory representations. Play with the reader's senses as well as your own. Visualize each stage of your story and describe it to your reader: what you see, hear, feel, taste, and smell. Make your readers feel what you feel.

- **Incorporate specifics that make the story come to life.** Bring in dates, times, places, and names. Make use of dialog.

- **Evoke emotions with strong characters.** Describe their actions and circumstances, thoughts, emotions, struggles, motivations, and triumphs. If you are the main character in your story, take care to avoid hubris. Your readers will empathize more with your weaknesses, obstacles, and hard-won lessons than with your achievements. Give the accolades to others: your mentors and supporters.

- **Make judicious use of literary devices such as metaphor, simile, and analogy.** A metaphor ignites associations in the reader's mind, welding a new concept to something they already understand. A simile is like glue, making your words stick in the reader's memory. An analogy facilitates comprehension in the same way that a wrench tightens a bolt. Words are tools for communication.

- **Toss in action verbs.** These entice readers to picture what's going on in the story. Action verbs grab readers at a kinesthetic level, enlivening the narrative and magnetizing attention.

With these elements, your readers will automatically make mental movies to accompany your story. They will visualize the sequences of events, "see" the characters, and form impressions and associations. They will feel emotions and sensations. They will develop a connection with you, the characters, and your message. They will understand the message. The more tangible your story is to you, the more it becomes real and evocative to your readers (Marshall, 1986).

Closings: Leave Readers with Something to Remember

Once you've established rapport with your readers, led them, and told them what to do, how do you say farewell in a way that makes your message memorable? Many writers end their works too abruptly, without a definitive farewell to the reader. A closing is intended to bring resolution, summarize your ideas, or give the reader something to think about. A good closing is like putting a ribbon on a gift package—it's the final touch. Here are some ideas for closings:

- The points you want readers to remember

- What you conclude from your analysis

- How the points of your message can be assembled into a coherent whole or a complete process

- The moral of the story

- A call to action

- A finale that harkens back to the opening

- A preview of what to expect next

- A cliff-hanger that leaves the reader in suspense until the next chapter or installment

- "The rest of the story …" The story behind the story.

- The questions that remain to be answered

- A final, thought-provoking question

- A story or example that illustrates the point

- The solution to a problem, mystery, or riddle you've presented

- The answer to a final question that might be on the reader's mind

- A short quiz that prompts readers to test their knowledge of your material.

- Parting words of wisdom

I close this chapter with a story about how I once captured a reader's attention and created instant rapport at the same time, getting exactly the response I wanted.

Some years ago I was looking for work. I'd been unemployed (except for my part-time practice) for about six months. I'd sent out about 70 résumés, inquiries, and job applications, without result. I applied to a small company advertising for a Program Manager/Writer. I had experience in both aspects of the position. All I needed was to convince the person doing the hiring that I was, indeed, the ideal candidate.

Noting that the company's address was near my home, I dropped by. I told the receptionist I wanted to apply for the job and asked for the name of the person to whom I should address the cover letter. Using a person's name, if you can obtain it, is always more personal than a "Dear Sir or Madam."

I usually started out my cover letters with the standard, "I'm writing this letter to apply for the position of … that you advertised in the

Washington Post ..." This time I decided to first establish rapport with the recipient. I decided to make my résumé cover letter stand out from all the rest.

Here's how I wrote my cover letter:

> Dear Mr. _____,
>
> Right now, you are, no doubt, going through a stack of applications for the position of Program Manager/Writer. I'm sure you are a busy person, and your task is time-consuming. I can save you a lot of time and effort. Put all the other applications and résumés aside. You need search no further for the perfect candidate. You are holding in your hand, right now, the résumé that you've been searching for. Read it and you will be convinced that my qualifications exceed your requirements.

They did. He did. I got the job.

CHAPTER 8

For the Critic: Evaluate and Revise Expertly

"Proofread carefully to see if you any words out."

William Safire

In the western U.S., when people speak about the California gold rush of the 1850s, an iconic image ambles into the mind. A grizzled prospector is kneeling beside a stream, his trusty pack mule nearby, laden with picks and shovels and the meager necessities of life in the open spaces. The prospector wears dusty leather boots and a weather-beaten broad-brimmed hat that shades his face from the noonday sun. He plunges a tin pan beneath the water, shoveling up sand and rocks. Then he swirls the pan in the water to rinse off the mud. Gazing intently into the contents of the pan, he carefully studies the sand and rocks in the sunlight, squinting, searching for a tiny glint—a gleaming nugget of gold.

When it's time to evaluate and revise your work, why not search for structural flaws, inconsistencies, mistakes, and awkward phrasing like a prospector panning for gold? When you find something to correct and revise, you could feel as though you've found a golden nugget!

So much better to catch your own errors before you release your work to others; they may find enough fault with it as it is. Nothing brings a writer more chagrin than finding a typographical, grammatical, or factual error after his or her work has gone to press. Yes, you can and should submit your work to the practiced eyes of a copyeditor and/or proofreader. Nevertheless, you should be the first to scrutinize your completed draft, because 1) you'll want the prerogative of choosing your own corrections and revisions, and 2) learning from your mistakes will improve your writing overall.

Evaluating and revising your work means changing hats. Take off the Realist hat and put on the Critic hat. With the often-difficult Realist work of developing and sequencing content, you cannot always judge the quality of your work objectively. In the Realist mode, you get close to the content, immersed in the flow of the narrative. When your draft is complete, it's time to become your own toughest critic.

Bring on the Critic!

What do you care about so much, that you want every detail to be perfect? Maybe it's a dinner party that you plan for favorite friends. Maybe it's a craft or hobby in which you take pride. Maybe it's the care you take with your appearance on special occasions.

Step into your own remembered perfectionist moment. Recall how it feels to attend to every small detail, searching for what's wrong or missing or out of place, eager to make corrections and improvements. Remember having the mindset that insists, "I will not be satisfied until I know I have done my best." Now you are accessing the Critic within. Anticipate that you'll apply this Critic mindset to every task involved in editing and revising.

This does not mean that you criticize yourself, but that you feel a compelling drive to make your draft into its best possible version.

As the Critic, you can now take on the role of the perfectionist, the stickler for details. You are the fussbudget who keeps editing and revising until everything is as good as you can make it. Like a hunter, you stalk the pages of your draft, your keen eye trained to seize upon errors, inconsistencies, gaps, confusion, and meaningless nonsense. You are now willing to question every decision, dissect each sentence, and double-check every fact. You are now ready to find fault, and to edit, correct, and revise with deliberation and delight!

Here's a warning: as the Critic, your task is to take your work from good to better to best. This is not the time to bewail your lack of talent or flail about, deriding the utter hopelessness and futility of your effort!

Perform Top-Down Analysis

Before getting wrapped up in details such as grammar and spelling, start the editing process with a top-down analysis. At this point, some writers print the draft and lay out the chapters on a large table, or tape the pages across a large empty wall, to see the work laid out in its entirety. Top-down analysis follows a sequence of steps working from the overall structure down to the smallest details. The steps are laid out here and in checklist form in the Chapter 8 worksheet in Appendix A.

Step 1—Evaluate Structure
First, evaluate the overall structure of your draft. Look it over, as many times as necessary, answering the following questions:

- Compare your draft to your original outline. Did you cover all the points?

- Do all the elements (i.e. sections and/or chapters) of the draft seem to fit together into a logical flow?

- Do the elements appear balanced? Do any parts seem underdeveloped or overdeveloped in comparison to the others?

- Are the chapters or sections uniform in size? Are any so large that they could be broken into two chapters or sections? Are any so small that they could be combined or expanded? Is there any material that should or could be moved to an appendix or an addendum?

If the above questions point to structural changes, make those changes now. Making structural changes means that you might add, delete or move entire portions of the text.

Once you've made structural changes, check any cross-references and correct for continuity. If you changed the cat story to a dog story in Chapter 5, remember to change the reference to that same story in Chapter 10. If you moved Chapter 6 to Chapter 8 position, remember to changes any references to that chapter accordingly, including the Table of Contents.

Step 2—Evaluate Content

Once you feel satisfied with structure, evaluate content. The questions below will serve as guidance (Hickman and Jacobson, 1997). As you move through these questions, don't make your edits right away. Just mark up the draft for any sections that need improvement. Specify with a margin note, highlight, different color of type, or sticky note what seems problematic or where improvements are needed.

- Did you support your thesis consistently throughout?

- Did you portray your author identity consistently throughout? Did you reveal too much or too little of who you are as the author? Did you come across to readers in the way you planned?

- Did you accomplish your original purposes? Do you find any content that seems superfluous or contrary to your purposes?

- Did you maintain your own particular perspective throughout? Did you tell your own story, in your own way, appropriate to the genre?

- Is there any content that might cause a problem later on (i.e. might be open to misinterpretation, might rapidly make the work unnecessarily outdated, might prove offensive to certain groups of readers)?

- Is your content relevant and comprehensible to your typical reader? Did you consistently maintain rapport with the reader? Did you use examples, vocabulary, and advice your reader will understand? For this evaluative step, shift places, again, with your reader. This time, however, take on the persona of a reader who is likely to question or disagree with anything you say. As you read over the content, ask questions such as: "So What? Why should I care? How do you know? Where's the proof? Why does this matter?"

Now that you've marked up the draft, go through it and revise. As you make changes, keep checking for continuity and consistency.

Step 3—Evaluate Sentence Construction

Sentence construction is the essence of correct grammar. Read through your document and check sentence construction. If you don't know how to diagram a sentence, I beg you to take a class in it or find someone to teach you. It is so essential to know how to identify a subject, a verb, adjectives and adverbs, direct and indirect objects, and prepositional phrases. It will save you a lot of editing headaches. At minimum, evaluate for any problems concerning:

- Subject-verb agreement

- Parallel construction within the sentence

- Proper placement of clauses and prepositional phrases

- Run-on sentences that could be broken down into two or more sentences

- Proper treatment of referential pronouns such as "it" and "these"

- Sentences that have more than one (unintended) interpretation, usually due to participles (e.g. Hypnotizing hypnotists can be tricky)

- Passive voice versus active voice

- Convoluted reasoning

Eliminate cumbersome wording that can bog down the reader. Make your sentences read crisply and smoothly. Don't use three words where one will do.

Step 4—Evaluate for Word Choice

Next, check for word choice. Here are a few pointers.

- Make sure you have chosen the word that conveys the exact meaning you want. For example, some people confuse the words "infer" and "imply."

- Check for overused words. Search a thesaurus for substitutes that add variety.

- Where appropriate, create images in your reader's mind by choosing colorful adjectives, vivid descriptions, and action-oriented verbs. Consider the difference between "She went down the street," and

"She whizzed right past us, her pigtails aloft, as she glided down the street on a pink skateboard."

• Replace time-worn clichés with something fresh.

Step 5—Check Style

If your work is a scholarly one, check the recommended style manual for your professional discipline, following the instructions for items such as headings, capitalization, punctuation, indentation, dates, equations, statistics, placement of tables and diagrams, and the use of proper nouns and official titles. The manual will also provide guidance on how to present citations, references, footnotes, endnotes, and so forth. If you don't have access to such a style manual for your profession, use a generic one such as Kate Turabian's *A Manual for Writers* (2007). If you plan on submitting your work to a publisher, ask which style guide the publisher prefers or recommends.

Step 6—Spell-check

Run a spell-check. Double-check the spelling of names and locations. Remember, your spell checker will overlook misspelled words that, nevertheless, make another viable word. If you typed "form" when you meant to type "from" your spell checker won't catch the mistake.

Step 7—Fact-check

Fact-check any item about which you are not entirely certain. Items most vulnerable to factual errors are equations, dates, statistics, locations, quotations, titles of other works, attribution (who said or did what), proper names, and professional titles. Additionally, take care to distinguish facts from opinions, unproven theories, assumptions, and conjecture.

Step 8—Evaluate Uniformity of Appearance and Layout

A publisher will take care of this step for you. For a self-published digital piece, such as an e-book, follow the seller's formatting requirements. For a non-published work, make certain that the appearance and layout of the finished draft is uniform throughout. Evaluate for consistencies and uniformity in the following:

- Lettering fonts and sizes
- Spacing before and after paragraphs; page breaks
- Use of bold type and italics
- Centered text; right or left justification
- Lists

This kind of analysis requires complete concentration. It is your quality assurance task. Take your time with every detail.

Clarify Meaning with the NLP Meta Model

The NLP Meta Model is an essential writer's tool for precision communication. It is based on the notion that communication is often not as clear and precise as it could be under ideal circumstances. People receive, process, and transmit information through their own unique "filters": their beliefs, biases, values, motives, and perceptions. Thus, even the most accurate and factual communication is, nevertheless, inevitably imprecise in these three ways:

1. **Deletions:** The information is incomplete, often leading to misunderstanding and confusion.

2. **Distortions:** The information is vague or contains abstractions, unspecified criteria, or unsubstantiated assumptions.

3. **Generalizations:** The information overemphasizes patterns or similarities to the extent that differences, distinctions, and exceptions are ignored.

The Meta Model is a method for inquiring about communication, developed for the purpose of detecting and challenging deletions, distortions, and generalizations; these are also called Meta Model "violations". Applied correctly, with curiosity, the Meta Model promotes understanding and specificity. The Meta Model is intended for conversational usage, but it also works for clarifying meaning and adding precision in written communication as well.

"Going meta" means that you look beyond the *content* of communication and examine the *structure* of the communication instead. When you understand a few basics of the Meta Model, you can notice the deletions, distortions, and generalizations in your own writing. In each instance, you can determine if the violation muddles the meaning you intended.

By asking and answering the right Meta Model questions, you'll know how to reword any sentence to clarify the exact meaning you want to convey (Hall and Bodenhamer, 2003). Now we'll examine each Meta Model distinction in more detail.

Deletions: To detect deletions, notice what is *not* said, what information is missing. Ask who, what, when, where, and why. For example, if you write the statement, "She left the house," you could add specificity by answering the following questions:

- Who is she?
- Who did she leave with?
- What did she take with her?
- When did she leave?
- Where was she going?
- Why did she leave?

Another type of deletion is the unsubstantiated judgment, which you can often detect in adjectives such as "good", "bad", "too much", "enough", "right", and "wrong." As an example, let's take the statement: "Sara was right to criticize Jake." You could ask, "Sara was right, in whose judgment, according to what criteria?" A broader question is, "How does one determine whether a criticism is right or wrong?" If you can specify how you arrived at your judgment, you add weight to your argument.

Distortions: One type of distortion is the "unspecified" noun, verb, adjective, or adverb. Unspecified words have fuzzy meanings and are difficult to interpret.

An example of an unspecified noun is "event", as in the sentence: "Joe attended an event." One question to ask is, "What type of event did Joe attend?"

An example of an unspecified verb is "tolerate", as in: "Meredith tolerates our beagle." One question to ask is, "What does Meredith do that indicates that she tolerates the beagle?" If you add specificity, your reader is more likely to picture and thereby understand what Meredith does when she is around the beagle.

An example of a sentence with an unspecified adjective is: "I drank a flavored soda." One question to ask is, "What flavor was it?"

An example of a sentence with an unspecified adverb is: "They went willingly." One question to ask is, "What did they do to indicate that they were willing to go?"

A good way to detect distortions is to ask yourself, "How do I know that?" If the answer isn't evident, then a distortion lurks somewhere.

Generalizations: One type of generalization is the "universal quantifier" that allows no exceptions. This type is easy to spot in words such as: "always", "never", "everyone", and "all". Take the statement: "Politicians always lie." You could challenge this by asking, "Do exceptions exist? Do politicians *always* lie? Does this statement apply to all politicians?" If an exception exists, then the sentence is factually false and open to dispute. You can solve that problem by qualifying the statement: "Many politicians have been caught in lies."

The Meta Model is especially useful wherever exactness and details matter: it is well-suited for describing processes, giving instructions, scholarly works, research papers, legal documents, crime scene reports, and explaining a rationale. It is less applicable to poetry, fiction, humor, creative writing, and when you want to leave some things to the reader's imagination.

While the Meta Model was developed for evaluating the precision of a single statement, bear in mind that writers seldom express their ideas in single statements. They build a case, develop a narrative, or describe a flow of events. Thus, the clarity of a single statement might be found not in the statement itself, but in the context of its paragraph, section, or chapter.

You'll find A Writer's Guide to the NLP Meta Model in Appendix B. The guide, shown as a table, lists the three Meta Model distinctions and their sub-distinctions, with examples of statements containing Meta Model violations and the questions to ask.

Take a Skeptical Reader's Position

In Chapter 7, you learned a simple process for taking your typical reader's perceptual position. Thus you learned how to appeal to your *typical* reader. Now, as the Critic, you can do something similar. However, this time, you take the position of a *skeptical* reader who is ready to question your logic and pounce upon the flaws in your thinking. This is how to become your own toughest critic.

Here are four positions a skeptical reader might take and how to counter each one:

I disagree with your premise.

When you make a case, especially concerning a controversial topic, consider the opposing viewpoint. Then, pre-empt it by establishing the parameters of your premise—where your idea applies and where it doesn't.

Here's an example: I published a short e-book on conflict resolution for couples—an instruction manual on how couples can stop arguing and reach agreements. A skeptical reader might have questioned how such simple instructions could remedy a couple's communication difficulties. I countered that skepticism in the introduction. I stated that my method would work best for couples in respectful, safe, emotionally supportive relationships based on mutual commitment. I recommended that couples who didn't succeed with my method could consider couples counseling.

How do I know you are telling the truth?

Provide proof that backs up your premise and assertions. In his highly-acclaimed book, *Influence* (1984), social psychologist Robert Cialdini examined various forms of social proof that lead to agreement, acquiescence, and compliance. He wrote that people tend to follow the example of others, especially when the guidelines for behavior are unclear. They accept what others do and say as social proof. Common methods of providing social proof include case studies, statistics, man-on-the street interviews, first-person accounts, testimonials, historical precedent, common practice, and endorsements by trustworthy individuals.

Cialdini also wrote that people tend to believe experts and authorities. To gain credibility, make sure that, somehow, your reader is aware of your credentials. Where you lack expertise, show that you have gathered information from credible sources: subject matter experts, scientific studies, government publications, and reference materials.

Your material offends my sensibilities.

We live in an age of "political correctness" that seems to breed a hair-trigger urge to "call out" statements that smack of prejudice and unfavorable stereotypes. Inspect your work carefully to eliminate anything that might inadvertently offend. State your opinions tactfully and diplomatically.

If you must say something that some will find offensive, one tactic is to admit that others will disagree and say why they might do so. Back up your statement with evidence that shows the merits of your position.

I don't understand.

Give your reader more than one way to understand your ideas. Use metaphors, analogies, examples, and graphics. For self-help books and instructional manuals, let the reader apply his or her learning through the use of quizzes, discussion points, and exercises. Give the reader a workbook or journal. Many authors now make their work available not only in print, but also through audio and video recordings. Some products combine media in a single package.

I hope the toughest test your writing will ever undergo will be the test you give to yourself in the role of the Critic. The next step is to submit your work to at least one other person whom you can count on for forthright feedback.

I know, I know. I'm speaking to you as though you aren't exhausted enough already!

CHAPTER 9

Get Feedback and Cope with Criticism

"Honest criticism is hard to take, particularly from a relative, a friend, an acquaintance, or a stranger."

Franklin Jones

Years ago, when I worked for a federal contracting company, I was occasionally assigned to a proposal committee. Each proposal committee was made up of various subject matter experts who would assemble a work/cost proposal in response to a federal "request for proposal" detailing work for which the government was willing to pay.

When the committee finished the draft proposal, we sent it to the firm's in-house proposal review team, affectionately known as the "murder" board. Their job was to, in effect, "murder" the draft by marking it up with red ink. They also bruised our egos by finding every weakness in the proposal that might lead to losing the contract bid. After the murder board review, our proposal committee would regroup to revise, correct, and lick our wounds. If we were working against a tight deadline, it often meant we kept working past midnight or over the weekend, before sending the proposal to the government procurement office.

Working on federal proposals was the first of my many experiences in getting feedback and criticism on my writing. Since then, I've received feedback and criticism from academic instructors, my dissertation committee, various readers, copyeditors, proofreaders and reviewers. My ego has been knocked around quite sufficiently. But what I've learned has made me a better communicator. I've also learned the value of humility: it allows me to listen when others evaluate my work.

If you want to write, an ability to handle feedback and criticism is essential to your continuing improvement. Any project you work on will benefit from a second pair of eyes on the page. That second pair of eyes is of no value, however, unless the owner of those eyes can catch your mistakes and suggest improvements.

The ability to handle feedback and criticism rests on two strategies. One is to respond resourcefully to criticism. The other is to recover quickly from a mistake. I'll discuss both strategies in this chapter. First, however, let's examine the many avenues by which writers can obtain feedback.

Feedback: How to Get it

The following paragraphs describe ways in which to obtain feedback on your work. The first two (submitting your project to a focus group or teaching a course or workshop) are options to take while your work is still in development. The feedback you get will help shape the direction of your project, identifying elements that will add to reader usability and appeal. You'll most likely turn to proofreaders, content readers, and subject matter experts when your draft is complete. A writers' group or a writing coach will critique your work at all stages of your project and lend ongoing, morale-boosting support.

Focus Groups: Writers who write for an industry often use focus groups to get consumer opinions of new products and marketing campaigns. Ad copywriters, for instance, might make up two or three versions of a single ad and ask a focus group to compare the versions and choose the one with the highest consumer appeal. Focus groups answer questions about marketability.

Script writers and movie makers sometimes submit their project proposals to focus groups for evaluation, before taking those projects into full-scale production. Focus groups are usually composed of people who share the demographics of the targeted consumer population.

If you are a solo writer, and especially if you plan to self-publish a book, you could form an ad hoc focus group from your professional affiliations. Civic organizations and community clubs might have members who are willing to serve as a focus group, in exchange for a speech, workshop, or free copies of the published work. With the availability of teleconferencing and online meetings, you can even assemble a virtual focus group.

Submit your proposal, outline, and sample chapters to your focus group. Ask for frank and unvarnished feedback and honest opinions. Since the purpose is to get as many views as possible, members should avoid censuring, or disagreeing with, each other. Ask the group what approaches and innovations would make your product sell. Ask about recommendations for marketing your material.

Teach a Course on Your Subject Matter: If your project is based on an instructional topic, teach it to a live audience before publishing it. Books often emerge from classroom courses and, conversely, classroom courses often emerge from books. You could ask a local civic organization or a professional training company to sponsor your course. You could teach your course through an education organization in your community, at a professional conference, or at your place of business.

Teaching your material to others will help you to organize it in a manner that others can most easily comprehend. You might discover ways to make it interactive through exercises and quizzes. Your students will give you feedback through their participation, questions, and evaluations of course content.

Proofreaders: When you've edited and revised your draft, your next step should be to find a proofreader. If you plan to submit your work to a publisher, it will not be well-received if it is full of errors in spelling and grammar. Publishers are disinclined to hold one's hand and teach high school grammar. I've coached writers with master's degrees who did not understand subject–verb agreement.

Unless you are a wizard at spelling and grammar, hand your work over to someone who is. That goes double if you are writing in a language that is not your native tongue. You can hire freelance proofreaders who will work by the hour. You'll find them on Internet websites such as www.Elance.com, www. Odesk.com, www. Freelancer.com, and www. Guru.com. A freelance proofreader is indispensible if you plan to self-publish because you (versus a publisher) are responsible for the quality of your final product.

Content Readers: Many independent writers routinely rely on a personally-selected, ad hoc cadre of readers to evaluate the quality of content. You could do the same. Your readers could be two or three trusted colleagues or friends. You could give them a questionnaire detailing the criteria by which you want them to evaluate your draft. You'll find a Reader Feedback Questionnaire in the Chapter 9 worksheet in Appendix A.

Some of the questions, of course, would depend on your genre. Nevertheless, at minimum, you could ask your readers to identify strengths and weaknesses, inconsistencies, points of confusion, omissions, unnecessary repetition, and inaccuracies. You could also ask them to identify anything that appears superfluous, pompous, trite, or offensive to anyone's sensibilities. I found a particularly thorough Manuscript Troubleshooting List in Jean Marie Stine's *Writing Successful Self-help and How-to Books* (1997).

Stine wrote about an author who threw a readers' party whenever she finished a manuscript. She printed out her chapters. Then she invited friends over and gave a chapter to each guest, asking for a chapter-by-chapter evaluation. Of course, she repaid her guests with ample food and drink.

Subject Matter Experts: Novice writers of scholarly books, research papers, and monographs often ask seasoned subject matter experts to read and evaluate their manuscripts prior to publication. Publishers, in fact, often call on subject matter experts to evaluate the merit of manuscripts by authors who are not, themselves, recognized experts on a particular topic.

My husband, John, co-authored his first book, a biography about a U.S. Navy officer who made his reputation when the U.S. was newly-formed. Commodore Charles Stewart, the book's central figure, served on the USS *Constitution*, during the war of 1812. While both authors were Navy officers and historians, neither had previously authored a book. They were delighted when a leading naval historian and former captain of the *Constitution* agreed to be one of their reader—evaluators. His imprimatur and subsequent endorsement added to the book's prestige at publication.

Join a Writers' Group: Local and regional writers' clubs and guilds provide meetings, forums, and newsletters that foster the craft of professional writing. Some groups have guest speakers who present on some aspect of writing and publishing. Clubs and guilds are also a place where writers can share their successes, setbacks, and personal accomplishments. Members can participate in online forums to learn about publishing and marketing, or to request critiques and opinions from other writers. They learn about resources, conferences, and educational events. Some groups are dedicated to a specific genre (such as romance novels or science fiction) or a particular author population (such as women writers). If you prefer a virtual group, search for a suitable discussion group on the Internet through social media and networking websites.

Hire a Writing Coach: A writing coach will help you at every stage of your writing project. A coach will help you set your production goals and hold you accountable for keeping commitments. He will team with you in working through sticking points. She will help you find the wherewithal in yourself to meet setbacks and challenges. He will encourage your motivation and creativity. She will edit and critique your work. Your money will be well-spent.

Responding Resourcefully to Criticism

Criticism is a form of feedback that is not always skillfully delivered and not always skillfully received.

How do you respond to criticism? Do you feel guilty or defensive? Do you feel victimized? Do you get angry with the person who delivered the criticism? Do you ignore it? While these types of responses are understandable, they are not the best ways to respond to criticism.

To respond resourcefully to criticism is to treat criticism as information. When someone criticizes you harshly, you could, of course, take it personally. Conversely, you could take it as a sign that the person criticizing is not communicating skillfully at that moment. You might actually disarm him by applauding his ability to speak up, even if you disagree with the message. You might calm her by agreeing with the parts of the criticism that seem valid, while disregarding or negotiating the other parts. By staying calm and detached, you could ask clarifying questions to get more information, rather than getting angry or defensive.

The NLP Responding Resourcefully to Criticism strategy (Andreas and Andreas, 1987 and 1989; Andreas, 1987) will help you to stay calm and collected in the face of criticism, while you regard it as information that may or may not be useful. The strategy is to actually *hear* the information, ask clarifying questions, evaluate the validity of the information, and then decide whether you want to act on the information.

The essential feature of the strategy is to stay *dissociated* while evaluating the criticism. Recall that to be "dissociated" means that you visualize the exchange as on observer, so that you can detach from your emotions. I recommend you mentally learn and practice the strategy, shown below, a few times so that you can apply it easily and instantly in real-life situations that you may encounter in the future. Give yourself about 20 minutes of quiet, uninterrupted time to practice the strategy. Here are the steps:

1. Briefly remember a time when you felt criticized and you responded with emotional discomfort. In your mind, recall the setting, sights, sounds, and the other person or people involved. Access the memory just long enough to remember what happened and how you felt.

2. Return your attention to the here-and-now. Take a few deep breaths and stretch to release any discomfort from that memory.

3. Take a dissociated view of that memory. Visualize a movie of yourself receiving that criticism. Now, you are the observer, watching yourself—over there, in front of you. Do whatever is needed to maintain the dissociation: make it appear far away, in black-and-white, or behind a clear, plexiglass screen.

Imagine the you-in-the-movie responding to the criticism in a resourceful manner, as follows:

a. Watch as the you-in-the-movie receives the criticism by hearing it or seeing it in writing, or maybe by seeing a disapproving expression on someone's face.

b. Imagine the you-in-the-movie calmly and objectively evaluating the criticism. You can make this part of the movie run in slow motion, if you wish. Visualize the you-in-the-movie visualizing the words of the criticism. See the words floating in the air in a "thought balloon."

c. Pretend you can hear the thoughts of the you-in-the-movie pondering questions and decisions about the words in the thought balloon. Here is what he or she is thinking:

"Is the person who criticized me a trustworthy source for this information? If so, I'll evaluate the criticism. If not, I'll tactfully disregard it."

"Is there anything in the criticism that I don't understand? If so, I'll ask questions for clarification. If not, I'll continue evaluating the criticism."

d. Watch the you-in-the-movie make another thought balloon; this one contains a hypothetical picture of what the critic has described. In other words, the you-in-the-movie is thinking, "If the critic is correct, here's how my behavior (or my result) would appear."

The you-in-the-movie evaluates the imagery, comparing what he or she knows with what the critic described. In this way, the you-in-the-movie evaluates the validity of the criticism with the question: "Is there any valid or useful information in this criticism?"

If there's no match, the criticism is incorrect. The you-in-the-movie decides to tactfully disregard the criticism. If there is a match, the criticism may contain useful information. The you-in-the-movie decides how to apply the information. The thought balloon disappears.

     e. Watch as the you-in-the-movie responds resourcefully and tactfully to the person who delivered the criticism.

4. Appreciate that the you-in-the-movie has learned a new strategy for responding to criticism. Reach out your arms and pull him or her into your body, so that you are integrating this new strategy into your repertoire.

5. Imagine a possible future scenario involving criticism from another person. Visualize that you receive the criticism. Ask yourself: "Is this critic someone to listen to?" If so, make a thought balloon of the words of the criticism. Do the words of the criticism accurately depict your behavior (or your result)? If you aren't sure, evaluate the criticism by visualizing what the words describe and comparing that to what you know about your own behavior (or the result). Is the criticism valid? Does it contain useful information? If so, what do you want to do with that information? Imagine how you could respond resourcefully to the person delivering the criticism.

6. Mentally practice applying this strategy in several possible future scenarios.

The goal of this strategy is to hear the criticism and determine if it emanates from a valid source that you want to acknowledge. The next step might be to gather more information about the criticism. Then, decide whether any information in the criticism is valid and useful. If so, the final step is to decide whether to take corrective action, as well as what corrective action to take.

Corrective action might entail an apology, an explanation, agreement, correcting a mistake, or a decision to change one's behavior in the future. The following diagram shows a flow-chart of the decision processes involved in Step 3 above, sub-steps a through e.

No one is perfect. Your writing will never meet with unanimous approval. There is no law saying that people shouldn't criticize you or that they should always agree with what you do. In fact, if someone does criticize your work, it could mean that you've succeeded in

Criticism Feedback

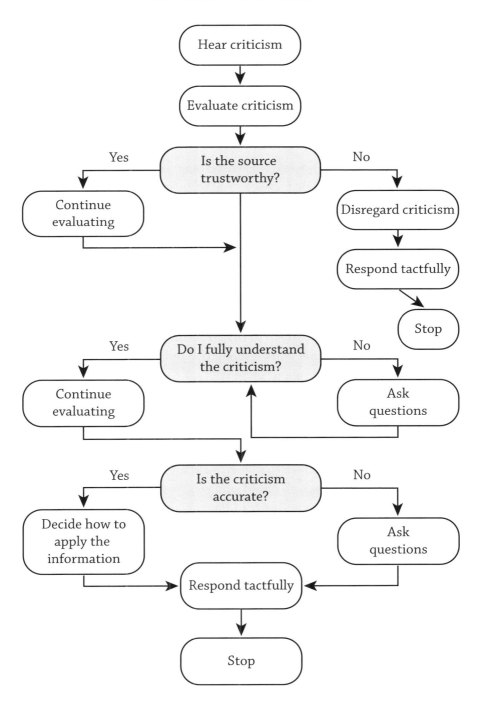

reaching a point at which people notice what you do and form opinions about it. People who receive the most criticism are often those who have reached the pinnacle of their careers.

There's no need to feel wronged by someone's criticism, or take it as a negative reflection of your worthiness. Anyone can make mistakes, offend another, or perform poorly. If the criticism is deserved, acknowledge the error, make amends, and follow the strategy for recovering quickly from mistakes in the next section of this chapter.

Even if you've made a mistake, exercised poor judgment, or performed poorly, there's no law that says you have to feel bad about it indefinitely. Feeling bad about it for five minutes is much more efficient than feeling bad about it for five days. If you can process the information in minutes, why spend days worrying about it?

After all this, if you still feel overly sensitive about criticism, perhaps it's time for reflection (Houghton, 2011). Ask yourself three questions:

- What meaning did I attach to the criticism?
- What did I think that person thought about me?
- What did I conclude about myself?

As you review your answers to these questions, ask yourself another question: "Are any of my answers true? Do my answers describe a permanent, pervasive condition about myself or about the other person?" You will probably discover that the critic may have been wrong, or unkind, but probably wasn't out to ruin you. You will probably discover that even a valid criticism does not apply across all your actions, but only to a single, isolated instance. The last question to ask yourself is: "What can I learn from this?"

Recover Quickly from a Mistake

Mistakes are inevitable. When you make a mistake does it wilt your confidence? When you make a mistake in front of others, do you feel awkward and embarrassed? If so, this next strategy will help you to acknowledge the mistake, take corrective action, recover quickly, and refocus on the task at hand. It might also boost your competence in the eyes of others.

The secret to recovering quickly is to acknowledge a mistake, make any necessary adjustments in your behavior, and then refocus. Again, give yourself about 20 minutes of quiet, uninterrupted time to learn the steps in this strategy:

1. Recall a time when you made a mistake and felt flustered, anxious, or embarrassed by it. Briefly recall what happened and how you felt.

2. Return your thoughts to the here-and-now. Take a few deep breaths and stretch to release the discomfort of that memory.

3. Visualize a movie of yourself making the mistake. Stop the movie just one second after the you-in-the-movie makes the mistake. Now change the scenario. This time, visualize the you-in-the-movie immediately acknowledging the mistake, "Oops! I made a mistake," or "Yes, I see I was wrong."

4. Next, visualize the you-in-the-movie wondering, "How shall I correct that mistake and get on with the task?" The you-in-the-movie quickly makes any necessary corrections, adjustments, apologies, or amends. Then he or she says, "That mistake is over and done. I put it behind me." Now he or she refocuses on the task.

   Reach out and pull the you-in-the-movie into your body, so that you are integrating this new strategy into your repertoire.

5. Return to the scene in Step 1, above. This time, associate into the movie. Play the movie through again with your new strategy. Make the mistake, pause, and acknowledge it. Ask yourself: "How shall I correct that mistake and get back on task?" Visualize that you are making any necessary corrections, adjustments, apologies, or amends. Say to yourself, "That mistake is over and done. I put it behind me." Imagine that you refocus on the task at hand and resume action.

6. Return your thoughts to the here-and-now. Mentally practice the strategy in Step 5 three to five times until you have memorized it and can apply the sequence in real-life situations.

If someone criticizes your writing and points out numerous mistakes, yet you aren't sure what to do to correct the problem, it's a good idea to get a second opinion.

A Second Opinion Won't Hurt

A colleague referred a client to me for mental health counseling. The man was a civil servant who had done well in his career of almost 20 years. His presenting issue was anxiety about finishing his master's degree thesis. Our initial sessions focused on how he could set his daily writing goals and remain calm and focused while completing each goal. That didn't help.

Then he revealed the source of his anxiety. His academic advisor refused to read his draft. When the client asked why, the advisor said, "It's garbage." I proceeded to work with the client on interpersonal communication skills: how to better tolerate criticism; how to approach his advisor with specific questions like, "What about my draft qualifies it as 'garbage'?" The client returned to my office more forlorn than ever. The advisor's answer: "Everything."

Neither the client nor I could understand how the advisor could be so disagreeable. I saw the client as the victim in this scenario. The counseling was going nowhere. My client's anxiety continued unchecked.

Finally, I had a bright idea, one I should have thought of earlier. I asked the client for a sample chapter. He readily complied. When I read it, I was astonished. It was rife with awkward wording, redundancy, poor syntax, incomplete sentences, run-on sentences, malapropisms, and inconsistencies. Each sentence compounded my confusion. My head was spinning after the first page! It was almost like reading a foreign language. How this man had gotten so far in his academics and his career was a mystery to me! No wonder his advisor had thrown up his hands in disgust! The client wasn't a victim at all. He was an abysmally poor writer!

He didn't need mental health counseling. He needed a writing coach! Little by little, over several weeks, we edited his draft. I explained and corrected each mistake, teaching basic rules of grammar, syntax, and sentence construction as our work progressed. The client insisted that no one had ever taught him these things. He had no inkling how terrible his writing was. I relieved him of that ignorance straight away.

Before our work was complete, my client had to relocate to another part of the country. He put his thesis on hold. Nevertheless, he said he was amazed at what he learned.

The moral of this story is, if someone dislikes or rejects your work, find out specifically where your submittal and their expectations part company. If you can't get that information, take your work to someone who can give a second opinion. If you learn that the problem lies in the clarity and quality of your writing, then take a writing course, hire a tutor, or get a writing coach.

CHAPTER 10

Write Hypnotically

"… the more you can meet your reader on the mental level where they are already preoccupied, the more you can create hypnotic writing that leads them where you want them to be."

Joe Vitale

"So for a few minutes, rest deeply and comfortably. Be interested in your own experiences as something that belongs to you, to be made available to you by your unconscious whenever you need them—not necessarily by name, but by a feeling of confidence that you can do this or do that; that you can understand things as they develop …" (Rossi and Ryan, 1985, pp. 131–132)

With words such as these, Milton H. Erickson could hypnotize one person or a room full of people, believers and skeptics alike.

Erickson, a psychiatrist, conducted hypnosis in a manner that was uniquely and exquisitely his own. Until Erickson gained recognition for his then-unorthodox hypnotic methods, most clinicians, if they practiced hypnosis at all, practiced "classical" hypnosis. That is, they told their patients what to do, directly and authoritatively. They used standard inductions and repetition: "Go to sleep, go deeply to sleep, deep sleep …" Few people responded well to that kind of hypnosis. Thus, the general belief was that clinical hypnosis had little therapeutic value because only a small percentage of the population was deemed hypnotizable. Erickson changed all that.

Erickson conducted hypnosis through casual-seeming conversation; often by telling rambling stories, philosophizing through examples and analogies, making seemingly irrelevant comments, sometimes speaking in puns or rhymes, and using vague, illogical, or confusing words and phrases. It sounded unusual, but his patients somehow achieved remarkable breakthroughs.

Eventually, "Ericksonian Hypnosis" eclipsed classical methods. During his later years and after his death in 1980, many considered Erickson one of the most influential hypnotherapists in the world. Since then, NLP practitioners and students of hypnosis have studied recordings, films, and transcripts of Erickson's hypnosis sessions to decipher his language patterns, analyze them, and replicate them in speaking and writing. In this chapter, we'll explore the theories behind hypnotic language (as influenced by Erickson), and methods for writing hypnotically.

Transderivational Search: Hypnotic Language and the Mind

Dave Elman, a contemporary of Erickson, and arguably one of the best-known classical hypnotherapists of the twentieth century, said of hypnosis that it "bypasses the critical factor" of the mind (Elman, 1964). He meant that, in hypnotic trance, people tend to suspend doubt, disbelief, and critical analysis—they tend to accept what they hear.

Hypnotic language is trance-inducing. It captures attention. It causes people to engage with the story and feel receptive toward the message. The hallmark of hypnotic language is that it automatically causes people to perform a mental process called "transderivational search." This means that people must search through their own memories and form their own associations in order to make sense of the words (Lankton, 2003). In doing so, they apply the message to themselves.

Transderivational search occurs when words sound meaningful within context, yet are vague and ambiguous enough to require a subjective interpretation. Erickson induced trance with words, phrases, and stories that stirred confusion and curiosity—thus evoking, in the listener's mind, a cognitive search to find the meaning, answer the question, solve the riddle, or resolve the confusion. When people focus inward in this manner, they must, out of necessity, screen out distractions and concentrate—entering a mild hypnotic state.

Hypnotic writing does something similar. It captures and holds the reader's attention. It makes the reader feel curious and intrigued. It evokes emotions through stories and images that grip the imagination. It makes the reader feel fully present in the moment, hanging on every word, eager to find out what happens next.

Hypnotic writing didn't originate with Milton Erickson, of course. It has existed ever since writers discovered that they could captivate their readers with stories and poetry. Pick up any piece of enduring fiction and there you'll see hypnotic writing.

The Psychology of Hypnotic Language: What Makes it Different?

John Burton is a masterful NLP practitioner, teacher, author, and Ericksonian hypnotherapist practicing in Greenville, South Carolina. He is a genius when it comes to hypnotic language. He has an unusual ability to make words charming, sensitive, and appealing.

He invents hypnotic metaphors based on everyday experiences such as driving a car, gardening, playing games, sitting in a classroom, fishing, travel, and telling time. These same metaphors are filled with symbols and analogies for behavioral change and problem solving: crossing a bridge, tending a garden, carrying an umbrella in case of rain, and shining a flashlight in the dark.

Burton has written two leading books on the structure and uses of hypnotic language. His analyses and brilliant explanations of the psychology behind hypnotic language are worth exploring in *Hypnotic Language: It's Structure and Use* (Burton and Bodenhamer, 2000) and in *Understanding Advanced Hypnotic Language Patterns: A Comprehensive Guide* (Burton, 2006).

So what is it about hypnotic language that makes it so effective and so different from language that is unambiguous and straightforward? Burton answers that hypnotic language affects the mind in three ways: 1) by stimulating our need to make sense of what we hear and apply it to ourselves, 2) by prompting our tendencies to organize and sort information and 3) by calling forth elements of child-like thinking. To explain all this, Burton draws from three sources: learning psychology, Gestalt psychology, and cognitive psychology. The following paragraphs summarize Burton's theories:

Learning psychology tells us that we consistently strive to make sense of experience. We are not passive receivers of information. Whatever we see, hear, touch, feel, taste, and smell, we decide what it means. Our minds process everything that enters our awareness. When presented with vague or ambiguous information, we bring our own meanings into it. We apply it to ourselves or to our own situation.

Gestalt psychology tells us that we continuously organize information into relationships and patterns to make all parts of that information into a meaningful whole (i.e. a gestalt). Whatever we perceive, we attend to relationships among the features. We look for similarities, contrasts, and inconsistencies We automatically organize, categorize, seek closure, make associations, and assign meanings. Hypnotic language takes advantage of these mental tendencies.

Cognitive psychology explores how we reason, solve problems, make choices, form judgments, assign value, and understand cause–effect. Burton draws from the work of child psychologist, Jean Piaget, who demonstrated that children's cognitive operations are different from those of adults. Children are less logical, less skeptical, less analytical, and more suggestible than adults, for example.

Burton theorizes that hypnotic language can incorporate elements of children's thinking, causing people to regress to childlike states. Storytelling is one way to do it. Reminding people of typical childhood experiences is another. With the openness of a childlike mind, adults might be more creative, imaginative, and open to new possibilities.

Would you like to read hypnotic writing that can transport you back to childhood? Read children's classics, such as *Charlotte's Web*, *Winnie the Pooh*, *Where the Wild Things Are*, and anything by Dr. Seuss. The best children's stories are written by authors who can think like children.

Adults enjoy reading children's stories to their own children because children's stories let adults feel like children again.

What Marketers Know

Perhaps the most popular book on writing hypnotically is *Hypnotic Writing* by Joe Vitale. If the name sounds familiar, he was one of the stars in the movie, *The Secret*. Vitale makes a portion of his living applying hypnotic language in advertising and marketing and in his many books. Hypnotic writing not only makes for engrossing reading—it's also perfect for selling (Vitale, 2007).

Actually, every writer could benefit from what top marketers know. To get published, you have to know how to write a winning query letter and a dynamite proposal. Even if you self-publish, you have to write advertising copy that motivates readers to buy your book. If you write for a business, you surely want to influence prospective customers. Hypnotic writing enhances your ability to persuade, motivate, convince, influence, and yes—sell.

Vitale states that hypnotic writing is "intentionally using words that guide people into a focused mental state ..." (p. 14)

Much of what Vitale advises, I've covered in previous chapters. To write hypnotically is to be in rapport with your readers, appeal to their senses, get their attention, and tell a good story (see Chapter 7). Here are a few more recommendations from Vitale worth passing along:

- Make your major points stand out with headlines, bullets, italics, and boxes.

- Use attention-getting headlines and subheads to make the reader want to know more and to serve as a road-map to steer your reader's interest.

- Activate the reader's imagination with stories, analogies, similes, vivid descriptions, and action verbs. Make your writing appeal to the senses, so that your reader can represent your words through memory, visualization, and association.

Consider, for example, which sentence has more impact: "Suppressed emotions are unhealthy," or "Suppressed emotions are like time bombs silently ticking away in your body."

- Create anticipation, suspense, and curiosity with a promise to reveal a secret, solve a problem, answer a question, teach a process, etc.

- Construct a "turning point": a story or narrative in which an individual encounters an epiphany, transformation, or redemption that ties in with your message, making it unforgettable.

Vitale advises that you apply hypnotic writing principles and tactics in the editing and revising stages of writing, polishing your work until you are certain readers will find it irresistible.

Sound Bites of Hypnotic Language

I've always felt so enchanted by hypnotic language that I started collecting bits of it long ago, assisted in particular, by the writings of Bill O'Hanlon (1987) and Richard Bandler and John Grinder (Bandler and Grinder, 1975; Grinder, DeLozier, and Bandler, 1977) all of whom extensively analyzed Erickson's work. Below are a few sound bites that seem well-suited to hypnotic writing:

- **Reversals of the Meta Model:** If you review the Meta Model (see Chapter 8 and Appendix B) you'll notice that deletions, distortions, and generalizations are often permissible in hypnotic language, especially when you *intend* to communicate with ambiguity and non-specificity. By leaving something to the reader's imagination, you help the reader perform transderivational search.

- **Presuppositions:** Make assumptions that you want the reader to accept, because those assumptions support your message. "When you think about it logically, you'll readily understand the implications of the policy." This sentence assumes that the reader can think logically, and by doing so, will immediately understand the implications—the exact ones which you are about to describe.

The Presupposition Formula: presuppositions often begin with these words:

When ... While ... After ... As ... Following ... "Following your arrival, you'll want a good meal." (Assumes you'll arrive and want a meal)

What will ... What is ... How will ...? "What will you say to her?" (Assumes you'll say something to her) "How will you improve your grades by next semester?" (Assumes the grades will improve)

I don't know whether ... I don't know which ... "I don't know which is worse, the winter or the summer." (Assumes both are bad)

- **Statements without any real attribution:** "Everyone knows ..." or "Experience shows that ..." or "Scientists tell us ..." An implied source increases the credibility of what you are about to tell the reader. "Medical experts tell us we should get eight hours of sleep every night." Such statements can also be a method for setting up a straw man argument, which you can then dispute. "Today, the majority of people will tell you that formal etiquette no longer matters, but I beg to differ."

- **Truisms:** Make obviously true statements about the reader's situation. "Right now, as you are reading these words, your eyes tracking back and forth across the page ..." Here's another example, a bit more removed: "We know how you feel at the end of the day. You're exhausted, you've had a grinding commute, and now you have to fix dinner ..." The purpose is to pace the reader's experience and then lead his or her thinking where you want it to go (Recall "pace and lead" from Chapter 7).

- **Yes-set:** Ask a series of questions to which the reader will certainly answer "yes". "Would you like to know just what to say to make a woman fall in love with you? Would you like to know the best way to get her to notice you?" The yes-set is a lead-in to a persuasive pitch, setting up agreement in the reader's response.

- **Pairing of opposites:** Combine two opposite meanings into a new idea. "It takes superb control to really let go of the need for control." Here's another: "He was confident in his timidity," and "Remember to forget this." This tactic contains an element of surprise, making it memorable.

- **Tag questions:** Ask for agreement with the previous statement. "Isn't that true?" or "Don't you agree?" Tag questions put the reader into an agreeable frame of mind, don't they?

- **Zeigarnik effect:** The Zeigarnik effect is a little-known psychological phenomenon coined after Russian psychologist Bluma Zeigarnik. It states that people tend to think about unfinished tasks more than finished ones. To create the effect in readers, tell them what to expect, but make them wait. "I'm going to tell you exactly how to increase your profits by 20%, but first …" This "cliffhanger" tactic creates suspense. Readers will keep reading, because they want to obtain what you promised.

- **Compounding:** A sentence that pairs two comparatives, such as more, less, better, worse. "The more politicians delay their decisions, the worse the economy gets." This tactic often implies cause-effect. "The hypnotic language patterns that are easiest to learn will give you the most advantage."

- **Illusion of alternatives (also called a double bind):** A statement that seems to give a choice that isn't a choice at all. "You can purchase the workbook online when you register, or order it from the distributor, or buy it when you arrive at the conference." The option to not buy the workbook is not offered. Either way, the reader must buy the workbook.

- **Cause-effect statements:** Cause–effect statements seem to provide explanations, yet they offer no evidence. They increase belief and often become self-fulfilling prophecies. Use words like these: Therefore … and that leads to … which causes … with the result that …

Cause–effect statements can be indirect or direct. An indirect cause–effect statement goes like this: "Make your work into a game and your creativity increases." Another example: "If you want to increase creativity, make your work into a game." A direct cause–effect statement goes like this: "Making your work into a game will cause your creativity to increase."

- **Indirect command:** This kind of statement tells people what to do, while seeming to not tell them. "You don't have to study any more than is necessary to pass the exam." Another: "You can eat anything you want, as long as you eat only lean meats, fruits, and vegetables." Here's one I like: "I don't need to tell you how important it is to get feedback on your draft before you send it to the publisher."

- **Stimulate curiosity:** Get the reader into a state of wonder or uncertainty. Use phrases such as: "Have you ever wondered … Doesn't it seem strange that … No one really knows … It's always been a mystery …" Example: "Have you ever wondered what it takes to write a bestseller?"

- **Trance-inducing statements:** Invite the reader to focus inward. Suggest experiences of visualizing, remembering, realizing, imagining, emotion, contemplation, surprise, revelation, insight, etc. "When you search inside yourself, somehow you know, at a very deep level, that the decision was already made long before you even realized it consciously. As you become aware of your own internal response, you experience that mental shift to clarity, surprised to realize just how much more determined you now feel."

Trance-inducing statements can also prove effective when written in the first person, inviting the reader to vicariously share the experience of the writer or the character through whom the writer is speaking. "My heart was beating. My thoughts were a jumble. I felt afraid and confused. I knew beyond any doubt I had to escape."

You can practice these hypnotic language sound bites with the Chapter 10 worksheet in Appendix A.

Be warned that editors, proofreaders, and other assorted sticklers for accuracy who are not schooled with hypnotic writing might, understandably, quibble with it, unless you explain what you are doing and why. On the other hand, perhaps they, themselves, will succumb to the enchantment of your words.

Take Your Writing into the Hypnotic Dimension

Hypnotic language is all around you. Soon you'll recognize it in movies, advertising, political speeches, and storytelling. By now, you might be wondering just how you'll begin to write hypnotically, while you realize that you might already be applying some elements of hypnotic writing without even being previously aware of doing so.

Hypnotic writing doesn't offer all the flexibility of speaking: pauses, inflection, accents, breath control, impersonations, and variations in volume, tone, and tempo. Nevertheless, applied judiciously, hypnotic writing might add a new dimension to your message.

Hypnotic writing lends itself to children's stories, self-help, inspirational, philosophical, fictional, fantasy, poetic, and narrative works. Well-chosen words that speak to the emotions and spirit, as well as to the mind, can heal wounds, expand possibilities, and transform lives. Hypnotic writing can turn words into magic!

The 1960s television series, *The Twilight Zone*, became a cult classic, its popularity due, in part, to the mesmerizing presence of the show's creator, Rod Serling. With the introduction to each episode, he seemed to cast a spell over his audience. The language and the visuals were a study in ambiguity. I've placed one such introduction at the end of this chapter for your enjoyment (you can find it on YouTube.com). This opening had Serling's smooth, masculine voice-over, and *The Twilight Zone*'s eerie musical theme playing in the background, while viewers watched a non-descript wooden door floating in a smoky void.

When you read the paragraph below, I suggest you imagine a door—a door to a treasure trove of new ideas for writing hypnotically.

You unlock this door with the key of imagination. Beyond it is another dimension—a dimension of sound, a dimension of sight, a dimension of mind. You're moving into a land of both shadow and substance, of things and ideas. You've just crossed over into the Twilight Zone.

CHAPTER 11

Write Prolifically

"It took me fifteen years to discover I had no talent for writing, but I couldn't give it up because by that time I was too famous."

Robert Benchley

NLP trainer, Richard Bolstad, knows a thing or two about writing prolifically. As a speaker, trainer, and international consultant, he is a man on the go. He holds the distinction of having trained more than half the NLP practitioners in his native New Zealand. In fact, he teaches for five international organizations on four continents. His central interest is in linking NLP to issues of spiritual development and interpersonal conflict resolution. In spite of his globe-trotting lifestyle, he has authored and co-authored numerous books, including my personal favorite: *Transforming Communication* (Bolstad and Hamblett, 1997). He has produced a multitude of articles, training materials, CDs, and DVDs.

In 2003, I saw an article by Richard: "How I Wrote over 100 Articles about NLP" (Bolstad, 2003). In it, he revealed many of the secrets and strategies behind his prolific writing. I kept rereading that article months and years after it first appeared in *Anchor Point* magazine. It inspired this book. You see, Richard writes according to the Disney Creativity Model (see Chapter 3). From that article, I first learned how to apply the model to my own writing.

Another element of Richard's success is that he writes from "a larger purpose": "Writing helps me reach thousands of people I'll never meet … Articles I wrote ten years ago are still being read for the first time by new people, often in languages I don't even speak … [I love] the excitement of sharing new ideas." (pp. 11–12)

Like Richard, prolific writers write for the joy of it. They feel a need to write as reliably as they hunger for food and thirst for water. Writing is indispensible to their sense of being.

In the literature and lore of NLP there is no specific formula for being prolific at anything. Nevertheless, NLP is, as you'll recall, a method for modeling excellence. By learning what prolific writers do, you can copy their methods and approach their level of acumen.

Since I began writing seriously over the last two decades, I've collected articles and books and attended workshops about writing and creativity by prolific, non-fiction writers whom I admire. When one of my favorite authors shares the secrets of his or her success, I sit up and listen. I take notes. I avidly read their books.

My goal is to model authors who, year after year, produce quality material well worth reading and who are willing to explain their strategies to novices. If you love writing and yearn to become prolific, I think you'll like this final chapter. It contains many of the best practices of prolific writers.

Make Your Writing Environment Efficient

As I mentioned in Chapter 1, every writer needs an environment in which to plan, write, and concentrate. Whether you work from home, in a rented office, or in a business or academic setting, you need an environment that offers comfort and efficiency. Even if your work requires travel and you pound out text on a laptop or cell phone, from an airport or hotel room, at some point, you'll return home. When you do, you'll want a quiet space, free of distractions, in which to finish one project and initiate the next.

Efficiency makes for productivity. Maximize efficiency in your workspace. For starters, make sure you have ample desk space, storage space, and shelves for books, supplies, and equipment. Set up a filing system (hard copy and/or digital) for business and marketing materials, as will as for reference materials. Assemble the office supplies you need. Keep them organized and close at hand. Where, oh where, did I put that stapler?

Build a reference library. Collect books, articles, and information products in your area of specialty or expertise so that you have a wealth of information at your fingertips. Periodically, purge your library of outdated material.

Evaluate your electronic equipment and digital needs. Writers of previous generations would go wild with envy if they could see the devices and software we use today! At minimum, you'll benefit from a high-speed Internet connection, flash drives loaded with gigabytes, a scanner, printer, copier, and fax. For the sake of your electronics, your space should have adequate lighting, ventilation, and electrical outlets with surge protectors. For the sake of your sanity get virus and malware protection and back up your digital files frequently.

Sigh heavily and commit to upgrading your electronics as needed. Persist in learning new technologies that ultimately give your work speed and flexibility. If you aren't technology savvy, find a good "techie" to consult with regarding your hardware and software requirements, updates, digital memory and storage requirements, and compatibility issues. You can hire such consultants on an hourly basis.

Additionally, locate a reliable computer repair firm that can remedy computer ailments with a quick response time. In a large metropolitan area, like the one I live in, a local computer help company makes house calls, thank goodness. Some computer stores will take in sick computers for repair and upgrade. Beware of unknown online companies offering a service whereby a technician can access your computer remotely to analyze and correct problems: you don't know about the integrity of the person who has now taken control of your computer and wants your credit card number.

Plan Your Work

For major projects, organize a work plan. Work plans are especially helpful for writing teams because a work plan ensures that everyone is on the same production schedule. At minimum, a work plan provides an estimate of the amount of time needed to complete a project and its components, so that you can schedule accordingly.

A good plan should list small, achievable milestones that lead to project completion. Break down your project into tasks that have logical start and stop points. Organize these tasks sequentially, allowing for some tasks to overlap or occur simultaneously. Project management software, such as Microsoft Project, allows a variety of options and formats for charting project tasks and milestones, allocating resources (expenses, time, and personnel), setting due dates, budgeting costs, and charting progress. If such charts are too complex for your needs, you can make your own simple work charts. Here's an example of a partial planning table for a book.

Activity	Start Date	End Date	Comments
Conduct market analysis			
Develop draft Table of Contents			
Outline each chapter			
Develop Research Plan			
Conduct research			
Write query letters			

An example of a simple milestone chart follows.

In this example, the line arrows show projected start and stop dates. The block, tinted arrows show when the actual work occurred. By

Activity	Jan	Feb	Mar	Apr	May	June	Comments
Conduct market analysis	→ →→						
Develop draft Table of Contents		→ →→					
Outline each chapter			→ →→				
Develop Research Plan			→ →→				
Conduct research				→ →→			
Write query letters			→→ ↓→				

comparing line arrows to block arrows, the author gets an indication of the accuracy of his or her planning estimates. Note that the hypothetical author was behind schedule most of the time, but did the query letters earlier than planned. She conducted research in a shorter time than estimated.

When milestones are shown graphically, overlaps and gaps become evident, possibly indicating where some tasks could be moved or shortened in order to accommodate the sequencing required. Your project may require finer granularity—say weeks or days, as opposed to months. With a milestone chart, you can estimate the days and hours needed for any given task. Then you'll be impressed with the need to manage your time.

Manage Your Time

If any writer understands time management, it's Bob Bly (not the poet, the copywriter). This freelance dynamo is a copywriter and marketing consultant to major corporations. He manages sales letters, marketing packages, press releases, white papers, annual reports, radio commercials, instruction manuals, business plans, website copy, newsletters, brochures and articles. He is also a writer's writer in that he has authored over 70 books and seminars on the business, technical, and logistical aspects of writing (Bly, 1998; 2006).

Bob Bly writes for non-fiction freelancers of all specialties. One thing you'll learn from him is that there's much more to being a successful writer than good writing. Successful writers are also business people who write proposals, respond to inquiries, speak at conferences, and negotiate contracts. To further complicate matters, many successful writers often work on multiple projects at varying stages of development. They collaborate with other writers, agents, editors, clients, and publishers. Bly has mastered the multiple facets of the writing business by writing prolifically and developing effective time management skills—and he teaches others how to do the same.

If you want to write prolifically, while performing numerous auxiliary tasks, and get paid, you will benefit from the following time management recommendations, many adapted from Bob Bly.

Realistically estimate the time you need. Chart time requirements for a given project and for multiple projects in various stages of development, so that you deliver on time. If you freelance, the ability to estimate the hours you need to complete a project will guide your fee-setting so that you are adequately compensated. Maintain a work plan on all current projects and check it daily.

Never commit to more work than you can handle. Never load your schedule to maximum capacity. Instead, leave room for unexpected delays or last minute changes in requirements.

Delegate routine administrative duties. If you freelance and can't afford a full-time secretary, hire a temp whom you can pay by the hour.

Pay outside professionals to handle business matters. Engage the services of a reliable bookkeeper, accountant, and attorney, all of whom will work by the hour. Hire a web designer if you need one.

Outsource routine work. Through the Internet, you can outsource routine tasks to other freelancers. Such tasks can include research, formatting, transcribing, translation, illustrations, and proofreading.

Do as much routine business as possible without leaving your office. Make use of online banking, phone calls, teleconferencing, videoconferencing, and email.

Minimize distractions. Turn off the radio and television. Limit visitors. Block out time each day for phone calls and email.

Work in one-hour blocks. In this way, you can divide up your work day and allocate time to various activities. One author I know writes for one hour, reads and journals for an hour, and develops teaching plans for an hour, four days a week, unless he is on the road, speaking and teaching. The rest of his day is dedicated to ad hoc and administrative activities. He spends one day a week marketing and networking.

Develop a work routine. Establish consistent work habits. It may seem impossible to set aside 100 continuous hours to complete a book draft. Instead, it's much easier to commit to writing for 60 minutes a day, five days a week. At that rate, under ideal conditions, you could finish that manuscript in five months. Some authors base their routine on word count. One author I know writes 1500 words every morning.

Learn the templates that suit your particular type of writing. Many types of writing adhere to a general template or outline. Proposals, research reports, press releases, how-to articles, business plans, and news stories are good examples. Writing to a template will save time because you'll know immediately how to organize your subject matter.

Develop or obtain formatted business forms. Save time with standardized formats for business contracts, customer questionnaires, proposals, policy statements, your bio sketch, permission requests, etc. In business settings, such forms are called "boilerplates." You'll use these forms over and over, tweaking them for each new project.

Establish priorities for your work. If you work on multiple projects, you need a guideline for deciding which projects to take on, scheduling your work on each one, and parceling your time. Give top priority to projects that meet one or more of four criteria: urgency, scope, impact, and pay-off.

- **Urgency** refers to a tight deadline. Urgent projects demand higher priority. Keep in mind that even if you have no specific deadline, your project may still have urgency if it is time-sensitive. Say, for instance, your topic is tied to a specific season, anniversary, or current event.

- **Scope** refers to the size of the project, in terms of the volume of words/pages and the amount of time required. Bigger projects may compete with smaller projects. While it's tempting to work on smaller, easier projects, you will want to set aside priority time for larger projects. Larger projects are seldom completed in one fell swoop. "Chunk down" cumbersome projects into smaller units and complete each project incrementally.

- **Impact** refers to the significance and meaning of your finished product. If you are writing a piece that could significantly affect many lives, then that piece warrants higher priority over one with less potential.

- **Pay-off** is the reward you get at project completion. Financial pay-offs might include advances, fees, royalties, or additional business. Less tangible pay-offs might include endorsements, testimonials, name-recognition, increased website traffic, marketing opportunities, speaking engagements, publicity, and opportunities to travel and meet influential people in your field. Give priority to the projects with the biggest pay-off.

Take advantage of "bonus" time. You arrive on time for the meeting, but now it is delayed for an hour. Your 2:00 pm flight has been delayed until 4:30 pm. The client who was scheduled to meet you at 9:00 called at the last minute to cancel, and now you have an hour before your 10:00 client arrives. "Waiting" time can be wasted time or it can be "bonus" time.

Take advantage of unexpected cancellations and delays by developing an ability to write on the go. Carry a notebook for jotting down ideas and composing new sections of your draft. Carry a laptop computer to write, edit, fact-check, send emails, and take care of online business. Dictate into a portable device such as a smart phone or digital recorder.

Schedule an occasional writing retreat. Temporarily take time away from other responsibilities. Assume the world will continue to revolve if you hide away for a few days. Notify clients, co-workers, and significant others as to where you'll be. Tell them you want no interruptions, except for emergencies. Stock up on healthy snacks. Go on a retreat where you'll focus your energies on writing.

Work with a co-author. A co-author can reduce your work load, especially if his or her expertise and skills complement and round out yours. Make sure your co-author has equal enthusiasm for the project and can meet deadlines reliably. Make agreements in advance about shared responsibilities, finances, payments and royalties, and ownership of the product and its spinoffs.

Network with other writers. Develop a network of trusted colleagues to consult with when you have a business or technical question and aren't sure how to proceed.

Keep the Ideas Flowing!

Many prolific writers write by assignment—they produce content "on spec". If you write strictly by assignment, you may not always like the subject matter, but you'll never run short on ideas.

If you develop your own content, the best way to keep the ideas flowing is to write about what you love and know and want to learn. Write about topics that pique your curiosity. Write about events that engage your values and emotions and reflect your philosophy. Write about what you want others to know. Below are 18 ways to keep the ideas flowing. The examples are fictional.

- Model a skill for others in a how-to, self-help, or do-it-yourself format. Describe your own skill or interview someone who has honed a special talent. Example: *So You Want to Do Stand-up! A Guide for Aspiring Comedians.*

- Describe a better way of doing something that many people already do. Example: *Nutritious Breakfasts in under 15 Minutes: Recipes for Working Parents.*

- Take an existing model or process and describe a new application for it. Example: *Social Media for Party-planning.*

- Develop an inspiring or fascinating biographical or historical account about a person or people who found a unique way to improve a process, contribute to others, solve a problem, or overcome adversity. Example: *Staying Together: How One Family Survived Homelessness.*

- Investigate the unforeseen consequences or little-known repercussions of current trends or newsworthy events. Example: *In Today's Economy, Some Women are Opting-out of Motherhood.*

- Explore the practical implications of a recent research study. Example: *A New Study Shows Obesity Contributes to Dementia: What this means for Baby Boomers.*

- Juxtapose two topics no one has brought together before. Example: *Meditations for Postal Carriers.*

- Expose a common fallacy. Example: *Autism is not a Mental Illness.*

- Reveal the history or origins of a current day product, organization, community, business practice, or social institution. Example: *The Early Days of Cough Medicines.*

- Document the antecedents of a historical event or scientific break-through. Example: *How America Decided to put a Man on the Moon.*

- Give several examples of a single characteristic or behavior demon-strated in unique or unusual ways by a particular group. Example: *Women CEOs of Fortune 500 Companies: Making it to the Top.*

- Predict what people can expect in the future if a particular trend continues. Example: *Gasoline Prices and the Future of Public Transportation.*

- Share a personal experience in which you encountered and solved a problem. Tell readers how they can apply what you learned and benefit from your experience. Example: *Our Son was a Bully: How We Intervened.*

- Discuss the reasons why people should or shouldn't follow a partic-ular course of action. Example: *Pet Health Insurance—Don't Buy It!*

- Tell an entertaining story with wit and humor. Example: *I Taught my Cat to Play the Piano.*

- Conduct research into a unique and little-known element of a his-torical event. Example: *How They Rescued Animals in the Aftermath of Hurricane Katrina.*

- Interview an accomplished figure in your field. Example: *An Interview with a Pulitzer Prize Winner.*

- Interview a person or group of people affected by a significant event or current trend. Example: *Interviews with Farmers Struggling through the Drought.*

- Construct an imaginary interview with a person of historical sig-nificance. Couch your questions regarding events of that person's era, or ask about that person's perspectives on current day events. Example: *How Would Winston Churchill Evaluate Today's Leaders?*

Write to Fulfill a Larger Purpose

The written word holds amazing power. It has the potential to ease suf-fering, instill hope, alleviate apathy, and expand the limits of perceived possibilities. Every work of writing begins with falling in love with an idea. Then it becomes the task of shaping and polishing that idea so that readers can also fall in love with it.

I've mentioned several writers on the pages of this book. All of them are prolific. They are talented, successful individuals who have immersed themselves in their subject matter. Although they are regarded as experts and authorities, I'm willing to bet that not one is driven by such recognition. For each one, writing is a way of life, a means of self-expression, an inquiry about the world, and a continuing quest.

Prolific writers write about something they deeply care about. They also care about honing their talents well enough that they can craft a meaningful message that engages readers. This desire to produce a work of value to share with readers takes writing to the spiritual level of experience that Robert Dilts described. With this desire, Richard Bandler and John Grinder wrote about Milton H. Erickson—and their anlysis led to the development of NLP. It's the reason L. Michael Hall "cannot not write." It fueled Disney's creative genius. It made Dixie Elise Hickman and Sid Jacobson formulate the POWER Process. It is Richard Bolstad's "larger purpose."

Writing is a medium for a message. Writing is a way of connecting with others by sharing one's passion. It's a way of influencing others through the impetus of an idea. It's a way of fulfilling *your* purpose. When you realize this about your own writing, *you* will become prolific.

APPENDIX A

Chapter Worksheets

CHAPTER 1 WORKSHEET

How Does it *Feel* to *Be* a Writer?

Logical Level Action Items

Below are six action items, one for each Logical Level discussed in Chapter 1. Select the action(s) that will most help you to experience what it feels like to be a writer.

Environment action item: If you haven't done so, set up the best writing environment you can. Choose a suitable location. Get the equipment, references, gadgets, and software you need for efficiency and productivity. Read more about a writer's optimum environment in Chapter 11.

Behavior action item: For a current project, make a sequential list of required activities, from start to finish. Estimate the length of time needed for completing each activity. Establish target start dates and end dates for each activity. Put them into a planning table like the partial one which follows. This will help you to identify the behaviors needed to complete the project and estimate the amount of time needed for each. See more about planning and time management in Chapter 11.

Capability action item: Look over your list of activities and tasks (the previous action item, above). Assess your skill levels for each one. What skills do you need to learn or improve upon? How will you do it? You could read a book, or attend a workshop, webinar, teleseminar, or writer's boot camp. You could hire a tutor or a writing coach.

Beliefs action item: Write down a single empowering belief that will reliably support your goals as a writer. Start with the sentence stem, "I believe …" Say it aloud. Visualize the fulfillment of this belief. Visualize

Activity	Start Date	End Date	Comments
Conduct market analysis			
Develop draft Table of Contents			
Outline each chapter			
Develop Research Plan			
Conduct research			
Write query letters			

this belief as a light that emanates from your brain down to every cell in your body, until your body is alight with the glow of it.

What is one decision you could make today that would inevitably emerge from this belief? What action will you take to implement this decision? When will you do it? Where will you do it? How will you do it? Plan it now. Act on your belief.

Identity action item: Locate a community of writers (or experts in your topic) with whom to associate. It could be an online community, a local group, or a national association. Participate, share, network, and learn.

Spirituality action item: Write a three-paragraph mission statement in the space below. In the first paragraph, describe your ideal readers, clients, or customers. In the second paragraph, describe how your writing benefits those kinds of people. In the third paragraph, describe a larger purpose for your writing. Keep these points in mind for inspiration.

My ideal readers …

_____

_____

_____

_____

How my writing benefits my ideal readers …

_____

_____

_____

_____

The larger purpose of my writing …

_____

_____

_____

_____

CHAPTER 2 WORKSHEET

Get Organized with the POWER Process Model

POWER Process Overview

Below, you'll see an outline of the POWER Process model. Use it to guide your actions through any writing project. The related chapters and worksheets (Chapters 4–9) for each step are shown in italics. If you need more information about completing any step in the process, simply turn to the designated chapter and worksheet.

Preview—Set the Stage for Your Idea

Chapter 4: For the Dreamer: Romance Your Idea
Chapter 4 Worksheet: Preview your Project

Self—Who are you as the author?
Purpose—What is the purpose?
Audience—Who is your target audience?
Code—How do you present your message?
Experience—What experience do you bring to bear?

Organize—Develop an outline

Chapter 5: For the Realist: Blast Past Writer's Block
Chapter 5 Worksheet: Make Your Outline

Write

Chapter 6: For the Realist: Get on Task and Stay There
Chapter 6 Worksheet: Reflections on Motivation

Chapter 7: For the Realist: Write for Your Reader
Chapter 7 Worksheet: Know Your Reader

Evaluate and Revise

Chapter 8: For the Critic: Evaluate and Revise Expertly
Chapter 8 Worksheet: Top-down Analysis Checklist

Chapter 9: Get Feedback and Cope with Criticism
Chapter 9 Worksheet: Reader Feedback Questionnaire

CHAPTER 3 WORKSHEET

Get the Right Mindset with the Disney Creativity Model

The Three Disney States

In the three sections below, write your own description of yourself and the activities you'll pursue in each state—Dreamer, Realist, and Critic—as applied to your current writing project.

As the DREAMER, I ...

_____

_____

_____

As the REALIST, I ...

_____

_____

_____

As the CRITIC, I ...

_____

_____

_____

For the Dreamer: Romance Your Idea

Preview Your Project

Now is the time to complete the first step of the POWER Process Model: Previewing. The five components of Previewing form the acronym: SPACE. Use this worksheet to preview your current writing project.

Self: What role and tone will you take as the author?

_____

_____

_____

Purpose: What do you want to accomplish with your project?

_____

_____

_____

Audience: Who are your readers and what are their needs and concerns?

_____

_____

_____

Code: What genre will best communicate your message? What medium (or media) is best suited to the final form your message will take?

_____

_____

_____

Experience: What experience do you bring to this subject matter? How will you compensate for any experience you might lack?

_____

_____

_____

CHAPTER 5 WORKSHEET

For the Realist: Blast Past Writer's Block

Make Your Outline

Having resolved any writer's block issues, organize your outline. Start with the major headings representing each chapter or section of your project. Under each, insert subsections or subtopics. If you aren't sure how to begin, develop your ideas with a mindmap or storyboard, as described in Chapter 4. List your major topics here, using extra paper as needed. Then proceed to develop a full outline.

Major Topic 1:

Major Topic 2:

Major Topic 3:

Major Topic 4:

Major Topic 5:

Major Topic 6:

Major Topic 7:

Major Topic 8:

Major Topic 9:

Major Topic 10:

CHAPTER 6 WORKSHEET

For the Realist: Get On Task and Stay There

Reflections On Motivation

Chapter 6 contains a number of NLP strategies for maximizing your motivation to write and stay on task. Having completed at least two of the strategies, examine your motivation. Reflect on your experience by answering these questions:

What is your overriding reason to write (you can list more than one)?

_____

_____

_____

What are the tangible and intangible rewards you expect from your current project?

_____

_____

_____

What is the value of your current project to yourself and to others?

_____

_____

_____

How to you visualize your goal that signifies the completion of your project?

_____

_____

_____

What self-talk will motivate you to write on a regular basis so that you finish your project?

_____

_____

_____

What will you do and think the next time you feel stuck, or your motivation lags, so that you will proceed with the task of writing, editing, and revising, as needed?

_____

_____

_____

CHAPTER 7 WORKSHEET

For the Realist: Write for Your Reader

Know Your Reader

Regarding your current project, think about it from your reader's point of view as you answer the following questions:

How would you describe your typical reader?

_____

_____

_____

How do you want your reader to apply the information you are providing?

_____

_____

_____

How will you convince your reader to accept your point of view?

_____

_____

_____

About what will you educate your reader?

_____

_____

_____

By what criteria will readers judge your work?

_____

_____

_____

What will make your treatment of the subject interesting enough that your reader will keep reading?

_____

_____

_____

CHAPTER 8 WORKSHEET

For the Critic: Evaluate and Revise Expertly

Top-Down Analysis Checklist

This checklist will serve as guide to evaluating and revising your draft.

Step 1—Evaluate Structure

❏ Compare the draft to the original outline to detect any inconsistencies.

❏ Check for logical flow of sections or chapters.

❏ Check for balance. Are any parts underdeveloped or overdeveloped?

❏ Check for uniformity. Are any sections or chapters too small or too large in comparison to others?

❏ Complete structural changes.

❏ Check and correct cross-references that may have changed. Consider chapter headings and chapter numbers, indexed words, and references.

Step 2—Evaluate Content

❏ Did you support the thesis consistently throughout?

❏ Did you portray your author identity consistently throughout?

❏ Did you accomplish your original purposes?

❑ Did you maintain your perspective and uniformly tell your own story in your own way?

❑ Is there any content that might be problematic (misinterpreted, rapidly outdated, or offensive)?

❑ Is the content relevant to readers' needs and expectations?

❑ Did you maintain rapport with readers?

❑ Did you use examples and language your readers can understand?

❑ Have you made the content meaningful to the skeptical reader?

❑ Have you offered convincing proof of your assertions?

Step 3—Evaluate Sentence Construction

Evaluate sentences for any problems concerning:

❑ Subject–verb agreement

❑ Parallel construction

❑ Proper placement of clauses and prepositional phrases

❑ Run-on sentences

❑ Proper treatment of referential pronouns

❑ Ambiguity

❑ Active voice versus passive voice

❑ Convoluted reasoning

❑ Wordiness

Step 4—Evaluate for Word Choice

❏ Check for similar-sounding words that are sometimes confused.

❏ Check for overused words and replace them.

❏ Add colorful adjectives, descriptions, and action verbs, as needed.

❏ Replace overused or outdated clichés.

Step 5—Check Style (scholarly works)

❏ Check headings, subheads, lists, and paragraph indentation.

❏ Check the placement, titling, and captioning of tables, diagrams, illustrations, and photography.

❏ Check use of proper nouns and official titles.

❏ Check formatting of footnotes, endnotes, citations, and references.

Step 6—Spell-check

❏ Check the spelling of proper names, locations, and titles of other works.

Step 7—Fact-check

Fact-check any item about which you are not entirely certain. Items most vulnerable to factual errors are:

❏ Equations

❏ Dates

❏ Statistics

❏ Locations

❑ Quotations (who said what, exactly—and possibly the circumstances under which it was said)

❑ Titles and authors of referenced works

❑ Professional titles and proper names

❑ Nationality of referenced individuals

❑ Whether referenced individuals are alive or deceased

❑ Attribution to the proper originator of a product or idea

Step 8—Evaluate Uniformity of Appearance and Layout

Check for the general appearance and layout of the following:

❑ Lettering fonts and sizes

❑ Spacing between sentences and before and after paragraphs; page breaks

❑ Use of bold type and italics

❑ Centered text; right or left justification

❑ Placement of inserted photos, maps, sidebars, graphs, etc.

❑ Use of white space

❑ Use of color

Get Feedback and Cope with Criticism

Reader Feedback Questionnaire

Give this questionnaire to content readers whom you have selected to evaluate and critique your work. This questionnaire will help them to understand the kind of feedback you want from them.

To the reader: Upon reading the author's draft, please respond to the items below, giving honest criticism and frank opinions.

Step 1—Evaluate Structure

Please evaluate the overall structure of the draft and write your responses to the following:

Did the structure seem balanced throughout? Indicate any parts that seem overdeveloped or underdeveloped.

_____

_____

_____

Comment on whether any chapters or sections seem too small or too large.

_____

_____

_____

Step 2—Evaluate Content

Please respond to the following items with respect to content:

Indicate any inconsistencies or contradictions in the author's message.

_____

_____

_____

Did you understand the author's purpose? Did the author accomplish the purpose? If not, indicate why not.

_____

_____

_____

Did the author portray a consistent identity and voice throughout? If not, describe the problems you detected.

_____

_____

_____

Please indicate any problems with the logical flow of the content.

_____

_____

_____

Did you detect any gaps or unnecessary redundancies in the content? If so, where?

_____

_____

_____

Indicate problems with any content that could be misinterpreted, rapidly outdated, or offensive to others.

_____

_____

_____

Did the author communicate in terms that you could understand? If not, what problems did you encounter?

_____

_____

_____

Did you get the feeling the author understood your needs and expectations? If not, how could the author relate to you, as a reader, more effectively?

_____

_____

_____

Did the author offer adequate proof of assertions? If not, where was the proof inadequate or lacking?

_____

_____

_____

Indicate any factual inaccuracies you found.

_____

_____

_____

Indicate any other general areas of content that could be improved.

_____

_____

_____

CHAPTER 10 WORKSHEET

Write Hypnotically

Hypnotic Language Practice

This worksheet will give you practice in constructing hypnotic language patterns around what you want readers to do or believe.

First, state exactly what you want readers to do or believe.

_____

_____

_____

For each hypnotic language pattern shown below, develop a sentence that supports what you want readers to do or believe.

Presupposition:

_____

_____

_____

Statement without any real attribution:

_____

_____

_____

Truism:

_____

_____

_____

Yes-set:

_____

_____

_____

Pairing of opposites:

_____

_____

_____

Tag question:

_____

_____

_____

Zeigarnik effect:

_____

_____

_____

Compounding:

_____

_____

_____

Illusion of alternatives:

_____

_____

_____

Cause–effect statement:

_____

_____

_____

Indirect command:

_____

_____

_____

Stimulate curiosity:

_____

_____

_____

Trance-inducing statement:

_____

_____

_____

APPENDIX B

A Writer's Guide to the NLP Meta Model

The NLP Meta Model is a tool for precision communication and lends itself well to editing and revising written works. It consists of three distinctions, describing the ways in which communication is imprecise. These distinctions are deletions, distortions, and generalizations (see Chapter 8); these are also called Meta Model "violations". Each distinction has sub-distinctions that further define the "flaws" in the communication under scrutiny.

Some of these sub-distinctions have odd-sounding names derived from the vocabulary of linguistics. Don't be put off by these names. You need not memorize them. It's far more important that you understand what to notice and what to ask to clarify meaning.

Each sub-distinction has its own type of questions that serve to bring clarity by recovering information that is deleted, replacing distortions with specifics, and tempering generalizations (Hall and Bodenhamer, 2003).

In the following table, you'll find the Meta Model distinctions that are most useful to written communication in three categories: deletions, distortions, and generalizations. Within each category, you'll find sub-distinctions (in bold type) in the first column. Below each sub-distinction, you'll see a few sample statements that illustrate the Meta Model "violation" in each sub-distinction. The second column shows sample questions to ask in order to challenge or clarify each statement. The third column tells you the purpose of the questions.

Distinctions and examples	Examples of the type of questions to ask to gain clarity	What the questions seek to do:
DELETIONS		
Simple Deletions		
I'm going.	Where/When are you going?	Recover information that has been deleted or left out (who, what, when, where, and why).
Sally said, "Hello."	Sally said, "Hello" to whom?	
I feel sad.	What do you feel sad about?	
I want to feel loved.	Loved by whom?	
Lack of Referential Index (unclear pronouns)		
They bother me.	Who are they?	Clarify the pronoun's reference (who, what, when, and where).
I want that.	What is that?	
It's wrong.	What, specifically, is wrong?	
I'll go there.	Where is there, exactly?	
Lost Performatives (unspecified value judgment)		
It's wrong to be late.	Wrong according to whom? What is the basis of lateness being wrong?	Reveal the determination of the value judgment.
He is a good husband.	What are the criteria for a good husband? By what standard do you make that judgment?	
Comparative Deletions (an unspecified comparison)		
We can do better.	Better in comparison to what?	Clarify the basis and extent of the comparison.
I do enough.	How much is enough?	
They want more money.	How much more?	

(continued)

Distinctions and examples	Examples of the type of questions to ask to gain clarity	What the questions seek to do:
DISTORTIONS		
Unspecified Verbs		
Joe manipulated me.	How, exactly did Joe manipulate you? What did he do?	Clarify the verb.
Unspecified Nouns		
I saw something.	What did you see exactly?	Clarify the noun.
Unspecified Adjectives		
He feels happy.	Happy in what way? How do you know he feels happy?	Clarify the adjective.
Unspecified Adverbs		
She learns slowly.	What indicates that she learns slowly? How does one measure speed of learning?	Clarify the adverb.
Nominalizations (nouns that substitute for actions)		
I want relaxation.	How do you want to relax?	Express the statement as an action, as opposed to an object.
I want his respect.	How do you want him to respect you? What behaviors would demonstrate that he respects you?	
Modal Operators of Necessity (verbs that indicate no options or choices)		
You must go now.	What will happen if I don't go now? Do I have an option to stay or to go later?	Determine the basis of the necessity. Recover any existing options or choices.
They should buy the blue car.	What will happen if they buy a car of another color? What will happen if they don't buy any car at all? Do they have a choice?	

(continued)

Distinctions and examples	Examples of the type of questions to ask to gain clarity	What the questions seek to do:
Modal Operators of Impossibility (statements of impossibility)		
It's impossible to solve that problem.	Is it impossible in every respect? Have you exhausted every possibility?	Recover the possibilities.
Either–or Choice (limits choice to only one of two options)		
Either she apologizes or I leave.	If she refuses to apologize, is leaving your only option? Are there no alternatives courses of action?	Expand the range of choices.
Mind-Reading		
I know he dislikes me.	How do you know? What brought you to that conclusion?	Recover the source or basis of the statement.
Complex Equivalence (a statement that A means B)		
When she frowns, it means she is upset.	How do you equate her frowning with being upset? How do you know it doesn't mean something else? What else could her frown indicate?	Examine meanings and inferences.
Cause–Effect (a statement that A causes B)		
He makes me angry.	How do you interpret his actions in such a way that you feel angry?	Challenge cause–effect statements.
Rainy days depress me.	What is your method for feeling depressed about rainy days?	
I'm shy because I'm short.	What do you tell yourself about being short that causes you to feel shy?	

(continued)

Distinctions and examples	Examples of the type of questions to ask to gain clarity	What the questions seek to do:
GENERALIZATIONS		
Static Words:		
People say that ...	What people specifically?	Challenge global statements to reveal specificity.
Science shows that ...	Which science specifically?	
Sports are ...	What sports specifically?	
Universal Quantifiers:		
Everyone hates me.	Everyone hates you? Every single person you know?	Challenge global statements to reveal exceptions.
You never listen.	Never? I've never listened one time?	
All politicians lie.	All of them? Always? You can't think of one exception?	

One of the difficulties of the Meta Model inquiry is that a single sentence can contain more than one Meta Model violation; thus inviting more than one question. The type of information you can obtain depends on the question you ask.

Consider the sentence: Teachers shouldn't use manipulation.

To recover the deletions ask:
- Teachers shouldn't use manipulation *on whom*?
- *When* should they not use manipulation?

To clarify the distortions ask:
- *How*, exactly, do teachers manipulate?
- They shouldn't manipulate *according to what rule*?
- What will happen if they *do*?

To challenge the generalization ask:
- *Which* teachers shouldn't use manipulation?

- Are there teachers who *should* use manipulation?
- Do *all* teachers use manipulation?

You could also challenge the presupposition by asking: How do you know teachers use manipulation?

The purpose of revising with the Meta Model is not that you have to clarify every nuance and subtlety in your language, but that you are alert to ambiguities and ways to make your communication more succinct.

References

Andreas, C. and Andreas, S. 1987. *Change Your Mind and Keep the Change*. Moab, Utah: Real People Press.

Andreas C. and Andreas, S. 1989. *Heart of the Mind*. Moab, Utah: Real People Press.

Andreas, C. and Andreas, S. 1991. A Brief History of NLP. *The Vak,* Vol. X. No. 1, Winter, 1991–92.

Andreas, S. 1987. DVD: *A Strategy for Responding to Criticism*. Boulder, Colorado: NLP Comprehensive.

Andreas, S. 2012. *Transforming Negative Self-talk: Practical, Effective Exercises*. New York: W. W. Norton.

Bandler, R. and Grinder, J. 1975. *Patterns of the Hypnotic Techniques of Milton H. Erickson, M.D., Vol. 1*. Cupertino, California: Meta Publications.

Bly, R. 1998. *Write More, Sell More*. Cincinnati, Ohio: Writer's Digest Books.

Bly, R. 2006. *Secrets of a Freelance Writer*. New York: Henry Holt and Company.

Bolstad, R. 2003. How I published 100 articles on NLP. *Anchor Point*, January, pp. 11–21.

Bolstad, R. and Hamblett, M. 1997. *Transforming Communication: Leading-edge Professional and Personal Skills*. Auckland, New Zealand: Addison Wesley Longman.

Brewer, R. L. 2012. *2013 Writer's Market*. Blue Ash, Ohio: Writer's Digest Books.

Burnham, B. and McCallum, J. 2006. *101 Reasons Why You Must Write a Book*. Sarasota, Florida: Profits Publishing.

Burton, J. 2006. *Understanding Advanced Hypnotic Language Patterns: A Comprehensive Guide*. Bancyfelin, Wales: Crown House Publishing.

Burton, J. and Bodenhamer, B. G. 2000. *Hypnotic Language: Its Structure and Use*. Bancyfelin, Wales: Crown House Publishing.

Buzan, T. 1993. *The Mind Map Book*. London: BBC Books.

Cameron-Bandler, L., Gordon D., and Lebeau, M. 1985. *Know How: Guided Programs for Inventing Your Own Best Future*. San Rafael, California: FuturePace, Inc.

Cialdini, R. 1984. *Influence: The New Psychology of Modern Persuasion*. New York: Quill.

Dilts, R. 1994. *Strategies of Genius*. Cupertino, California: Meta Publications.

Dilts, R. and DeLozier, J. 2000. *The Encyclopedia of Systemic NLP and NLP Coding*. Scotts Valley, California: NLP University Press.

Duggan, W. 2010. How Aha! Really Happens. *Strategy + Business Magazine*, Issue 61. Available at http://www.strategy-business.com

Elman, D. 1964. *Hypnotherapy*. Glendale, California: Westwood Publishing.

Grinder, J., DeLozier, J., and Bandler, R. 1977. *Patterns of the Hypnotic Techniques of Milton H. Erickson, M.D., Vol. 2*. Cupertino, California: Meta Publications.

Hall, L. M. 1995. *The Spirit of NLP: The Process, Meaning, and Criteria for Mastering NLP*. Bancyfelin, Wales: Anglo-American Book Company.

Hall, L. M. 2000a. *Dragon Slaying: Dragon into Princes (2nd edition)*. Grand Junction, Colorado: E. T. Publications.

Hall, L. M 2000b. *Secrets of Personal Mastery*. Bancyfelin, Wales: Crown House Publishing.

Hall, L. M. 2001. Games Prolific Writers Play. *Anchor Point*, April, pp. 21–26.

Hall, L. M. and Belnap, B. R. 2004. *The Sourcebook of Magic: A Comprehensive Guide to NLP Change Patterns, (2nd edition)*. Bancyfelin, Wales: Crown House Publishing.

Hall, L. M. and Bodenhamer, B. G. 1997. *Time Lining: Patterns for Adventuring in "Time."* Bancyfelin, Wales: Anglo-American Book Company.

Hall, L. M. and Bodenhamer, B. G. 2003. *The User's Manual for the Brain, Volume II: Mastering Systemic NLP*. Bancyfelin, Wales: Crown House Publishing.

Hickman, D. E. and Jacobson, S. 1997. *The POWER Process: An NLP Approach to Writing*. Bancyfelin, Wales: Anglo-American Book Company.

Houghton, A. 2011. Handling Criticism. *Reflections and Tips*. email Blog #51, September 9, 2011.

James, T. and Woodsmall, W. 1988. *Time Line Therapy and the Basis of Personality*. Cupertino, California: Meta Publications.

King, S. 2000. *On Writing: A Memoir of the Craft*. New York: Scribner.

Lankton, S. 2003. *Practical Magic: A Translation of Basic Neuro-Linguistic Programming into Clinical Psychotherapy*. Bancyfelin, Wales: Crown House. Publishing.

Marius, R. 1998. *A Writer's Companion (4th edition)*. New York: McGraw-Hill.

Marshall, S. A. 1986. Storytelling: Dressing Up Your Words. *The Toastmaster*, January, pp. 8–11.

McDermott, I. and Jago, W. 2001. *The NLP Coach*. London: Piatkus.

O'Connor, J. and Seymour, J. 1990. *Introducing Neuro-Linguistic Programming*. London: Mandala.

O'Hanlon, B. 1987. *Taproots: Underlying Principles of Milton Erickson's Therapy and Hypnosis*. New York: W. W. Norton.

Pearson, J. E. 2011. An Interview with Roy Hunter. *International Hypnosis Research Institute E-newsletter*, October.

Rock, D. and Page, L. J. 2009. *Coaching with the Brain in Mind*. New York: John Wiley and Sons.

Rossi, E. L, and Ryan, M. O. 1985. *Life Reframing in Hypnosis: Milton H. Erickson, Vol. II*. New York: Irvington Publishers, Inc.

Stine, J. M. 1997. *Writing Successful Self-help and How-to Books*. New York: John Wiley and Sons.

Strunk, W. and White, E. B. 1999. *The Elements of Style (4th edition)*. Boston: Allyn and Bacon.

Turabian, K. L. 2007. *A Manual for Writers of Term Papers, Theses, and Dissertations, 7th edition: Chicago Style for Students and Researchers* (Booth, W. C., Colomb, G. G., Williams, J. M, eds). Chicago: University of Chicago Press.

Vitale, J. 2007. *Hypnotic Writing: How to Seduce and Persuade Customers with Only Your Words*. New York: W. W. Norton.

Wycoff, J. 1991. *Mindmapping: Your Personal Guide to Exploring Creativity and Problem-solving*. New York: Berkley Books.

Copyright Acknowledgments

I wish to thank the following authors for their permission to adapt, cite, and/or quote their work:

Steve Andreas and Connirae Andreas for permission to adapt the NLP Responding Resourcefully to Criticism pattern (in my Chapter 9) found in *Change Your Mind and Keep the Change*, 1987, and *Heart of the Mind*, 1989, both published by Real People Press in Moab, Utah. This material can also be found in the DVD: *A Strategy for Responding to Criticism*, 1987, Boulder, Colorado: NLP Comprehensive.

Richard Bolstad for permission to quote (in my Chapter 11) from his article: "How I published 100 articles on NLP", in *Anchor Point*, January, 2003, pp. 11–21. I also thank him for writing the foreword to this book.

John Burton for permission to summarize his outstanding work on hypnotic language patterns (in my Chapter 10) taken from his two books: *Understanding Advanced Hypnotic Language Patterns*, 2006, and *Hypnotic Language: Its Structure and Use* (with Bob Bodenhamer), 2000, both published by Crown House Publishing, Bancyfelin, Wales.

Robert Bly for permission to cite his work in my Chapter 11, Write Prolifically.

Robert Dilts for permission to adapt his work on Walt Disney (in my Chapter 3) taken from *Strategies of Genius*, 1994, Cupertino, California: Meta Publications.

L. Michael Hall for permission to quote his article, "Games Prolific Writers Play" from *Anchor Point*, April, 2001 and for his permission and help in explaining the Mind-to-Muscle pattern (in my Chapter 6) found in *Secrets of Personal Mastery*, 2000, Bancyfelin, Wales: Crown House Publishing.

Dixie Elise Hickman and Sid Jacobson for granting permission to develop an entire chapter around *The POWER Process*, which they published in 1997, with the Anglo-American Book Company. Without their generosity, I could not have written this book.

Roy Hunter for allowing me to publish (in Chapter 6) a previously unpublished excerpt from an interview I conducted with him in September 2011.

Ernest Rossi for permission to reproduce a quote by Milton H. Erickson (in my Chapter 10) taken from *Life Reframing in Hypnosis: Milton H. Erickson, Vol. II*. 1985, New York: Irvington Publishers, Inc.

Joe Vitale for permission to cite his work (in my Chapter 10) in *Hypnotic Writing*, 2007, New York: W. W. Norton.

I am richly blessed to have a connection with these writers through their work. Their generosity in sharing their knowledge is a gift I cherish. I feel fortunate to share these gifts with my readers.

Index